Praise for *Hearing His Whisper*

"Lauren pulls back the hospital room curtain and invites us into her intimate conversations with God when everything was on the line. It's a body and soul makeover you'll never forget. God turns the ugliness of life into indescribable beauty. Read and believe."

—Jack Crabtree, Executive Director, Long Island Youth for Christ, Long Island, New York

"Experiences so deeply painful and personal, like being diagnosed with, and fighting breast cancer can be eased by others. In Lauren's book, she shares her breast cancer experience in the unique form of her prayers to God, and Jesus' responses to those prayers. Lauren's writings helped ease my own battle, and truly reassured me of the love God has for me."

—Smyth Colwell, Massage Therapist, Colorado

"This extraordinary book takes you through the intense battle against breast cancer and the fight for survival. Along the way, you will hear the cries of suffering, the promises of the Bible, and the compassion of God bringing His child into new life. A rebirthing story written from the heart."

—Dave Garrison, Psychotherapist, Colorado

"Lauren is Jesus' Velveteen rabbit. Her soul is the artwork of Jesus, and all her beauty is bundled into love, grace and mercy which radiates through the words contained in this book."

—Candice B. Rossi, MSN, OCN, Adult Nurse Practitioner, Hematologic Malignancies, Blood, and Bone Marrow Transplant Program, University of Colorado Hospital

"*Hearing His Whisper* is a great read! A well-written, very inspirational book that brings the bible to life allowing the reader to enter into the experience of communion with God in a very unique way. Lauren's choice to continually seek out the beauty in the midst of pain witnesses to the power of positive thinking and its healing benefits, emotionally and physically."

—Dr. Paul Seligman, Professor of Medicine University of Colorado

"Adversity is a language that all people speak, and Lauren Miller talks eloquently with God about her troubles hearing hope and consolation in return. Listening to God speak in this book will be heard by all who suffer, loss, pain, and rejection."

—Rev. Andrew Kemberling, V.F., Pastor, St. Thomas More Parish, Centennial, Colorado

"I can only say, 'I totally recommend Lauren Miller's empowering words and wisdom to anyone who loves to read words that inspire, connect, and sound like amazing poetry from the heart.' "

—Tammy Cunningham, Life & Spiritual Coach, Heart Intelligent, LLC, Denver, Colorado

HEARING HIS WHISPER

HEARING HIS WHISPER

WITH EVERY STORM JESUS COMES TOO

●●●

LAUREN E. MILLER, M.Ed.

EDGE GD IN PRESS

Published by Edge God In Press
www.EdgeGodIn.com

Hearing His Whisper, 3rd Edition
©2025 Lauren E Miller. All rights reserved.

No part of this publication may be reproduced, stored in a retrieval system or transmitted in any way by any means, electronic, mechanical, photocopy, recording or otherwise without the prior permission of the author except as provided by USA copyright law.

For permission contact Lauren at info@LaurenEMiller.com

The Thompson Chain-Reference ® Bible New International Version, Copyright © 1983 by The B. B. Kirkbride Bible Company, Inc. and The Zondervan Corporation. Used by permission. All rights reserved.

Cover design & Book format by DocUmeant Designs
www.DocUmeantDesigns.com

Published in the United States of America

First Edition 2008 by Tate Publishing, LLC.

For inquiries about volume orders, please contact:
Lauren E Miller at info@LaurenEMiller.com

ISBN: 978-0-9994172-5-6 (print)
ISBN: 978-0-9994172-6-3 (epub)

1. Inspiration: Journals & Diaries 2. Biography & Autobiography: Personal Memoirs08.09.26

DEDICATION

● ● ●

This book is dedicated to my mom, Kay Miller, who laid down her life for a time to help save mine . . . I will cherish holding your hand through so many nights for the rest of my life.

ACKNOWLEDGMENTS

• • •

To my *A-Team:* My amazing dad, who always sees the rainbows in the midst of any storm, my selfless sister, Kimberly; Deano, you continue to captivate my heart daily with your gentle love and support; my beautiful children: Kaylin, Johnny, and Kimberly; my amazing brothers, John and Tyler; my sister-in-laws, Aunt Dale, and my entire family. Amy, Leslie, Stina, Carrie, Lynne, Lu, Linda, Carla, Kami, Ellen, Sandy, John, Amanda, Sue, Tommy, Alicen, Dave, Susan, Brenda, all of my neighbors and friends, my nurses, doctors, and surgeons. Thank you for reminding me that my soul still has hair, that once you become real, you can never become unreal, that there is a way to navigate trauma back to inner peace, for helping this story of victory through the storm come to life, reminding me how to get back up after being knocked out, that nothing thrives in a state of war and all things are possible for those who believe, for believing that if I survived it was because of my Jesus, reminding me whose ultimately in charge here, for urging me to go to go to the doctor when my right side broke open from a MRSA, sepsis infection, for walking me into intensive care unit, for paying the driver $200 in the midst of a snow storm in order to get to my bedside, for choosing to remain and love this family that is not biologically yours, for looking beyond the scars and baldness and seeing the beauty within me and reminding me that mirrors rob the soul of its true identity and taking care of my children, sending cards, cooking meals, making phone calls, giving embraces, watching me as I slept, holding my hand through the IVs, moving in with me, visiting me, taking me to the hospital over and over and over again, singing to me, praying with me, talking to me, listening . . . for hours, Holy Communion, crying with me, washing me when I was too weak to wash myself, planting the beautiful flower garden in my name, racing with my name on your back, expressing how beautiful you thought I was bald and breastless, reading to me when I couldn't read for myself, shaving your head and eyebrows so I wouldn't feel alone in my baldness, flying out to see me many times when you had three young children to care for because you picked up on the unspoken loneliness and desperation in my voice, overcoming your fear of flying because I needed someone by my side, covering all of my mirrors when I wasn't ready to look at myself, picking me up off the floor after I fainted, filling my days with robins. For all of the gifts, music, laughter, and love . . . I acknowledge the inspiration and strength that flowed through your hands and hearts into mine. It is because of your love for me, put into action, that these words flowed so easily from my heart through my pen . . . I am eternally grateful.

    A special thanks to Alicen Halquist, my friend and top trauma therapist. Thank you for seeing my need to work through unresolved trauma from the storm. For providing a safe space for me to navigate my way through the strong emotions and beliefs that were still stuck in my "earth suit" and I didn't even know it until I started to revisit the scenes. You are a gift from God for such a time as this.

CONTENTS

Dedication
vii

Acknowledgments
ix

Foreword
xiii

Preface
xv

Introduction
xxix

Before
1

Pictures
136

During
141

After
215

St. Theresa's Prayer
217

Three Simple Songs
218

About The Author
225

FOREWORD

•••

People often share their life stories. And often we listen closely as they tell them, not only because there is something in us that loves a good story but because their stories reflect back to us something of our own story. Universal truths about human life are encapsulated in a single life's story. We glimpse in that one tale the mutual fears, the common courage and wisdom, and perhaps a shared faith in God.

I am a man, and I have never faced a life-threatening illness. But in Lauren's story, the story of a young mother in the throes of a divorce facing the horrors of breast cancer, I glimpsed the fears that sometimes haunt my nights. I saw a courage and wisdom that evoked courage and wisdom in me. But more than anything, I witnessed a profound and honest faith in God that refreshed my faith.

I have known Lauren Miller for nearly twenty years. Her autobiographical and devotional journal is extraordinary for at least two reasons. The first is the story itself. This is the jolting narrative of a beautiful young woman and devoted mother who did it all right—lived healthily and faithfully—yet was suddenly confronted with both divorce and a potentially deadly form of cancer. Her faith meets the grit of life head-on; that alone makes these pages gripping.

But Lauren draws the reader into that story with a gripping trialogue—a candid three-way conversation among herself, scripture, and the voice of Jesus. The result is an intersection of radically personal diary and fresh devotional writing that reflects back your own fears and faith, your own courage and wisdom.

—Michael L. Lindvall
Author of *A Geography of God: Exploring the Christian Journey, The Christian Life: A Geography of God, Good News from North Haven,* and *Leaving North Haven*
Senior Pastor Brick Church, New York City

"But blessed are your eyes because they see, and your ears because they hear. For I tell you the truth, many prophets and righteous men longed to see what you see but did not see it, and to hear what you hear but did not hear it . . . but what was sown among the thorns is the man who hears the word, but the worries of this life and the deceitfulness of wealth choke it, making it unfruitful. But what was sown on good soil is the man who hears the word and understands it. He produces a crop, yielding a hundred, sixty or thirty times what was sown" (Matthew 13:16–17, 22–23).

PREFACE

• • •

Back in 2006 I was diagnosed with advanced cancer one week prior to my final divorce court date. In less than a two-year period of time Jesus carried me through a divorce, a double mastectomy, sixteen chemo treatments, one year of additional chemo, six weeks of daily radiation, fourteen surgeries due to third degree burns on my chest they had to graph my back onto my front (so now I really don't know if I am coming or going most days), and a MRSA staph infection that caused my body to go septic. I experienced two near death encounters in the midst of it all.

Hearing His Whisper was written before 2006 and contains my conversations with Jesus about every day frustrations and wonderings about life before, during and after what I call now as my best educational accomplishment: A PhD in Suffering. Jesus once told me to remain attentive in the trial because God does His greatest work in the eye of the storm.

After re-reading through the pages of *Hearing His Whisper* (first edition, 2009) before re-launching it out into the world, I felt a sense of WOW! Along with a profound gratitude that I am still wearing this "earth suit". Eight years later I can say with full confidence that with every storm Jesus comes too. There has never been a moment that I was left empty handed when it has come to God's faithfulness and grace to move my mountain. In the midst of the hardship, tears, fears and self-doubt our God reigns. As Jesus said in this world we will have troubles AND in the midst of those troubles Jesus encourages us all to take heart because he has overcome the world. YAY! YAY!

So, what exactly does that mean? Increase your confidence when faced with a storm, emotional bump or animal planet moment in life for with every inconvenience and heart break, for those who ask, seek and knock, a greater space for faith, confidence and love begin to emerge and cast out fear, doubt and worry. God is the great worry overcomer and strength finder. Why should we be surprised that it is through the experience of suffering that we regain the ability to give our soul permission to guide our flesh in all things? Suffering is the archway through which salvation was birthed into this world.

Jesus spoke clearly to me about this in the midst of acute pain: "Don't resist that which can transform you instantly out of self-focus into God centered. Suffering and the surrendered life walk hand in hand, free from the yoke of slavery." My prayers these days flow from a simple request based on John the Baptist prayer: "Increase my desire to love serving others, being small and rejoicing in the success of those around me over my own because that's when you will be BIG in me. Override my need to be right, liked and understood and close the gap in my ability to hear and respond to your whisper behind me saying, 'this is the way, walk in it.'

Since the original publication of *Hearing His Whisper* I have been blessed with several rainbows in my life. My three beautiful children who were 8, 10 and 12 back in 2006 are now 26, 28 and 30, happy faith-filled and healthy. I've been blessed with 4 grandchildren The lessons they learned throughout the experience of suffering have lingered with them into all facets of life including a deep compassion and desire to serve those in need. I kneel before there now empty rooms as I entrust them to the one who carried us all through the storms of life as they spread their wings and fly. He is faithful and will do 'it' whatever our 'it' is God is Jehovah-jireh and He provides.

I got re-married to a man, Dean, I had a crush on when I was a freshman in college. He had never married; my close friend re-introduced us in 2007. I remember the night my friend called me as I was driving home from Biblical School urging me to stop by and meet him. My reply was an easy no: "thanks for thinking of me but this is not the time to be dating I am trusting God to help me save my life."

She didn't take no for an answer and pulled out the Holy Spirit card. She said: "I really feel like the Holy Spirit is moving me to introduce you guys."

I still pushed back: "I'm bald and breastless this is not the time to start dating." Obviously, that didn't end up sticking, the next thing I knew I was on our first date sitting at a sushi bar.

This is how that rolled out. I ended up stopping by the restaurant my friend was at only to find her sitting at a table with a bunch of guys. They were having a meeting together to send medical equipment to third world countries, which is cool. I had my wig on and my pads in, so no one could tell what I was going through, in fact a few of the guys gave me their cards. I remember laughing inside thinking: *"I could really freak these guys out right now if I said: man, it's hot in here and pulled off my wig."* I've always asked the Holy Spirit to give me the gift of joy and laughter knowing that if I have that, I can handle anything.

When I wasn't looking, my friend asked Dean for his card, and she slipped it into my pocket. There was a moment that evening when everyone left the table, leaving Dean and I looking at each other. He leaned in and said: "Hey, check out that couple over there, you can totally tell that this is their first date. He's playing with the silverware wondering what to say next." I thought to myself: "hmm, this guy is a deep-sea diver, I like that, he's perceptive and picks up on the unseen." When I got home that evening I found his card in my pocket and called up my friend: "Hey I appreciate you introducing me to Dean he seems like a nice guy but still not a good time to date my friend." To which she replied: "Trust me on this, I feel like God wants you to connect, at least pray on it and don't throw his card away." So, I did.

One afternoon when I was working on this book, I glanced at Dean's card, which I placed next to my computer, and felt the Holy Spirit prompting me to reach out. I took a deep breath and started a short email: "Hey, it was nice to meet you perhaps our paths will cross again." Within less than a minute I got a reply: "How about dinner Thursday night."

I remember laughing as I was getting ready the night of our first date as I put my wig on and pads for my chest feeling like I was dressing up for a costume party. We met at a Sushi bar and I ended up running into my neighbors which was a bit awkward, yet they were so excited I was out.

Dean and I kept saying that we both looked familiar, like we have known each other before. After connecting with each other on a bunch of different topics we discovered that we knew each other in college. My sorority and his fraternity did song fest together. He was the main singer and dancer for the heat miser song. He was a senior and I was a freshman. We both had secret crushes on each other, and he taught me how to swing dance and do the pretzel. As soon as we discovered this it was like a domino effect of emotions and memories flooding my heart and mind as we reminisced together. I started to panic as reality crashed in about my current condition. I went inside my interior castle (as St Teresa of Avila calls our inner world with God) to seek wisdom. Instantly I heard: be "transparent." I instantly pushed back on that one: "no thank you." A few minutes later, the message popped in again: "be transparent." Once again, I pushed that back up to God. A third time the message came in loud and clear: "BE TRANSPARENT" and along with it a tailender that moved me to action: "fear not, for I am with you."

I took a deep breath and jumped in with: "Hey, listen this may sound a little odd on the first date, but God is moving me to be completely transparent with you so here goes: I can tell already that I like you and would love to spend more time getting to know each other. It's important that you know where I am in my life . . ." I paused and took a deep breath and said in my inside voice: "Here I go Lord". I continued on with: "Just so you know I am going through the experience of advanced cancer, I am bald and breastless, this is a wig, and these are fake pads for my chest. I have three beautiful children, I went through a divorce a year ago, I am in the midst of chemo and surgeries and I have to know if that is a deal breaker?"

As soon as I got my truth out in the open I quickly retreated back into my castle: "There Lord, I did it." I could feel Jesus just smiling all over me. After a long pause, I could see my now husband, then first date, slowly eye balling my wig. He then blurted out: "Wow! That's a wig? You can't even tell, I had no idea. What a great wig." Then he took a quick glance at my chest and said, "don't worry about it, I'm a leg and butt man." We both burst out laughing and that was that.

We dated for 2½ years, taking our time and allowing God to heal and restore as a family and had a Big Fat Greek wedding on October 3, 2009. I will often ask him if he ever truly felt like running away as fast as he could when I shared with him my situation and he always responds with: "It never crossed my mind, God told me to stay."

Our God restores what the locust have eaten. God is in the repair and restoration business there is no project in our imperfect lives that is beyond the healing ability of the great carpenter, whose hands and heart were pierced out of love for us.

There were several times throughout the eye of the storm when I didn't think I would make it through the night. I came across a journal entry recently that I did not include in the first addition of *Hearing His Whisper* and felt it was timely to insert into this edition of *Hearing His Whisper:*

Lord if I leave this earth tonight and you welcome me into your arms I want to leave the gift of death bed wisdom. This is my prayer: "Instill within each human being the wakeup call that occurs when you are faced with a terminal illness without actually going through it." This call invites you to align yourself on a daily basis with what you value most. This call teaches you to love first, then lead. To put people before things, linger in beautiful moments in life that cause you to pause in the midst of your "to do" list. This call expands your ability to surrender all to God with the faith and trust that flows from knowing you have been gifted another day of life and with that comes an urgency of living, loving and being present in the gift of each moment.

This call gives you the ability to release your need for certain outcomes in order to know you are enough or that you have already "made it" in life. Attachments, expectations and assumptions no longer drive your ship. Love, positive connection and moments of kindness take over your actions and intentions. The need to own, control, possess, analyze, interpret and conclude are released leaving you with endless opportunities to create in order to inspire.

Jealousy and comparison are no longer on your radar; you rejoice in your own gifts and talents and offer that gift to those around you. A sense of entitlement is replaced by a profound sense of gratitude for every breath and heartbeat you are graced to experience each day. Love and confidence become your best friends enabling you to ask for what you want, forgive and release, accept what is and change for the better what can be changed. This call allows you to accept people where they are without judgment, including yourself, no longer needing others to see things the way you do or respond and interact with life the way you do, your purpose for living becomes very clear: to grow in the ways of love and kindness on a daily basis, love better today than yesterday, experiencing a confidence in the beautiful creation you are that is so expansive you forget about yourself and lose yourself in the One who died to win your heart and attention.

You find your life, perhaps for the very first time, in the experience of losing all attachments except for one: your heart to God. In this space of new life with and through Christ you reconnect to a limitless supply of energy to create beauty and inspiration in the world wherever you are led to go. You embrace the reality of Galatians 5:1, "It is for freedom that Christ has set you free. Stand firm them and do not allow yourself to be burdened by the yoke of slavery."

I want to share a story with you that offers a remedy to help lighten the load of hardship and suffering almost instantly when applied.

I've carried this wisdom with me to this very day and offer it to you dear reader to make it your own. I remember one day I was going through a particularly difficult chemo treatment and a friend of mine invited me to go see one of Mother Teresa's nuns, Sister Rosalie who happened to be in town. She came and picked me up, I was very week and emotionally low. Sister Rosalie was about 5 feet tall and could have been a sister of Mother Teresa, she was blessed with the experience of working side by side with Mother Teresa in Calcutta India. She asked me how she could pray for me, and I lost it. Everything spilled out of me all over the place, crying as I declared all the fears and setbacks that I was experiencing. She looked up at me with profound compassion and said something that literally course corrected my entire perception of my trial: "Don't waste your suffering." I stopped crying and asked what she meant. "Don't waste your suffering, lift it up for the sake of salvation of souls, for those who are suffering even more profoundly than you are in this moment. Something miraculous happens within your soul when you make a prayer that flows from your hardship, just as it did for Jesus when He hung on the cross. He prayed for all of us. As we work with the poorest of the poor, our mission is not to save them from their suffering, it is to offer them love in the midst of it all. Love heals all wounds." I carried this wisdom with me and applied it immediately that night when my body was twisting and turning from the chemo. It was miraculous, as I prayed for others amid my own pain, the peace of God replaced the emotional turmoil linked to my own suffering. God never wastes our suffering, rather, He uses it for a greater good when offered up in faith, than had the trial never occurred. We see examples of this in nature: the rose amid the thorns, the rainbow in the eye of the storm, the peace that passes all human understanding in the life of someone who chooses faith over fear. Are you facing a challenge or trial today? Invite the Holy Spirit to teach you the lesson, strengthen character, remove fear, increase courage, expand compassion…God loves you right where you are at and loves you enough not to leave you there. For more encouragement in this area visit: EdgeGodIn.com, explore the series entitled: Don't Waste Your Suffering. My dear friend Joni Eareckson Tada shares her amazing story of faith over fear in this series.

As an executive coach, trainer and facilitator of learning I am consistently seeking out new fun ways to make the complex simple, applicable and sustainable. Upon the completion of my Master's Program in Adult Education, Emphasis in Human Resource Development from Rutgers University, through God's grace and creativity I have created a simple model of learning, which offers a quick methodology to unlock sustainable learning in life personally and professionally. I was moved to include this in the re-launch of *Hearing His Whisper* as a container through which you, as the reader, can highlight and pull along into your life those pieces of information that the Holy Spirit sparks in your soul.

The intention behind the L.O.V.E. to Learn Circle is to simply raise your awareness around four phases of content absorption and application that will help you take what sparks your interest in life and apply it quickly to champion your personal excellence in Christ. Since creating it I have increased my noticing around information that has value to me followed by an intention to integrate it into my daily life. As with any suggested theory or model in life, take what offers value and opportunity for you and release the rest.

Miller's L.O.V.E. Learning Circle™ for Sacred Scriptures:

Miller's L.O.V.E. Learning Circle™

L: Learn & Listen: Pause and invite the Holy Spirit into your experience of reading the Sacred Scriptures. Be attentive to content that is meaningful and adds value to your life experience personally and professionally.

- What's in this verse or reflection for me that will add meaning to my life and champion me into the person God has created me to be in this world?

O: Observe: Seek out 1–3 gold nuggets of wisdom (theme thoughts) that add value and meaning to your personal relationship with Jesus and the witness of His love through you. What sparks my attention and desire to learn more? Journal and proclaim what the Holy Spirit is saying to you as you pause on those verses and reflections that weave in with your personal journey of life and capture your attention. Ask:

- What specifically about this verse or reflection has caused me to pause and reflect?

- What moved me away from my fears, doubts and worries into trust and confidence in God's presence and guidance in my life?

Observe and Write down your theme thoughts: *short phrases, which capture a specific idea.* For example: *"Do not conform to the pattern of this world but be transformed by the renewing of your mind"* (Romans 12:2). Step away from the world: power; possessions; popularity and allow God to transform your thinking. Write 1–3 theme thoughts down you wish to integrate into your daily life.

Theme Thoughts from today's Hearing His Whisper scripture and message:

1. _____
2. _____
3. _____

V: Visualize: Visualize integrating the meaningful verses and messages into your daily life. What do you look like, feel like, sound like as you identify and adjust your thoughts, perceptions and behaviors to align with the guidance and insights you have attained through your reading and time with God? Use your imagination to ignite the emotions you will feel as you visualize more of God and less of you. *(St. John the Baptists Prayer)*

The conscious mind does not know the difference between real and imagined. Use this gift to strengthen your awareness of the fruits of the Holy Spirit in your daily life. Do you want to see more love and kindness in your life? Ask the Holy Spirit to remind your mind of what you look like, feel like and sound like when God's love moves you to be kind and loving. Whatever you focus on will grow BIGGER.

E: Explore: Explore specific forward actions steps you will commit to taking in the coming days and weeks to integrate the new learnings into your words, thoughts, deeds and actions as you move into making God recognizable in your daily thoughts, words, deeds and actions. Explore and journal about what you will notice to be different in your life as a result of applying the insights given to you through the Holy Spirit into your day-to-day interactions personally and professionally.

Today I choose to take the following positive forward action steps; supporting my desire to integrate what the Holy Spirit has revealed to me in my theme thoughts:

Action Step 1. _____

Action Step 2. _____

Action Step 3. _____

Close in prayer using your own words or integrating the following prayer:

"Dear God, you woke me up today for plans to prosper me, to give me a hope and a future. I give you permission to have your way with me in spite of myself because I know that your ways will bring me the fulfillment and inner peace and confidence I seek. My greatest joy comes in the measure through which I serve. Reveal to me my service project for today. Open the eyes of my heart and the ways of my

mind so that I resurrect my ability to step away from shiny objects, which distract my heart from the mission for which it beats. I choose you over the ways of the world. Come into my heart and be the Lord of life: my words; thoughts; deeds and actions. I want to make you recognizable in this world."

INTRODUCTION

• • •

I practiced Tae Kwon Do for 17 years and ultimately achieved, by God's grace, a double black-belt. During that time, I trained up for the Colorado World Tae Kwon Do State Championship. Master Kwon was my trainer who was an eighth-degree black belt from Korea who was also a believer in Jesus. He had many words of wisdom throughout the years. Master Kwon was all about the inner game of life. Giving more authority to the strength of God within you than the circumstance outside of you. Stress is the power we give to outside circumstance to define what we believe we are capable of handling successfully in life. When we give more authority to the circumstance than to our belief that the strength of God within us is greater than the situation at hand, we render ourselves vulnerable to rising and falling depending upon how we perceive the world is judging us at that time or how big the storm is that we face. When David faced Goliath in 1 Samuel 17:48, it says that David ran towards the battlefield line. How did he do that? He believed that the strength of God within him was bigger than the Goliath he faced.

At the World Tae Kwon Do Colorado State Championship I was paired with someone from the University of Colorado's team who was much younger than I was, which caused me a bit of anxiety. Master Kwon picked up on my stress and invited me to focus on my skillset and God's strength within me. However, when the referee blew the whistle at the beginning of the first round, I was knocked out by an illegal back hook kick to my head. As the referee counted down: 10, 9, 8, 7, 6, 5, …when he got to 4, I opened my eyes and realized what had happened. I remember thinking to myself: "There is no way I am going down like this, not after practicing 4 hours a day 6 days a week for a year." I felt this anger in my gut which catapulted me to my feet, and I went after my opponent like a spider monkey. I ended up winning a silver medal. As my ego escorted me off the podium, Master Kwon came up to my face and said, "you lost Lauren, you let your skillset get hijacked by your emotions, you lost focus and what you practiced." He was right, my emotions hijacked my skillset. I had spilled out of myself and lost all focus. Not the first time that has happened to me and it was certainly not the last, yet I will never forget that lesson: don't let your emotions be the boss of you. Give God more authority within than the circumstance outside of you so that you remember what you have learned and practiced outside the ring. Success in the ring of life is a direct result of the practice you put in outside the ring.

This is particularly true when it comes to spiritual warfare. I had the opportunity to interview Father Vincent Lampert, author of the book Exorcism (if you are looking for some light reading, haha), on our Edge God In Podcast (EdgeGodIn.com: Spiritual Warfare Wisdom from an Exorcist). He shares 4 ordinary activities of the devil used every day to bump us out of the peace of Christ: Deceive, Divide, Divert, Discourage. The devil **deceives** us and has been since the garden wanting us to question if we can trust

God, to **divide** us, pit us against each other, in order to **divert** our attention from God's mercy, love and guidance in order to **discourage** us. Discouragement is the devil's ultimate desire. It's essential for success in the spiritual ring of life to know your opponent so that you are prepared to replace the lies with God's truth. As I went through the dark night of the soul, I experienced all the ordinary activities of the devil, serval times over. Perhaps you can relate. Cool thing is: *"For everyone who has been born of God overcomes the world. And this is the victory that has overcome the world – our faith"* (1 John 5:4), and wait there is more: *"But thanks be to God, who gives us the victory through our Lord Jesus Christ"* (1 Corinthians 15:57).

I was physically knocked out in the ring prior to 2006, yet I had no idea the knockout I was about to experience several years later.

The voice on the other line said, "Lauren, are you sitting down?" The tone sent chills through my body.

"Yes," I said, still hoping it was a wrong number . . .

"Lauren, you have cancer . . . you have Invasive Ductile Carcinoma grade three." Everything in my body began to shake. I was trembling so severely that I could barely hold the phone as the nurse began to give me the details of what my future would look like battling stage-three breast cancer under forty. I was told that I had a 50/50 chance of survival.

That was January 10, 2006. I was thirty-eight years old, a mother of three children and in the middle of a divorce. In fact, my divorce was going to be finalized two weeks after I found out I had cancer. Looking back almost one year later, I felt as if I was surveying the damage of a natural disaster like Katrina—except it happened to my body. My new hair was frizzy and very short, yet I had coverage and I was very grateful for that . . . my breasts . . . well, I wanted to go out and get a shirt that said, "Under construction. Unit available January of 2008." That summed it up for me. Truth is I am under construction, physically, emotionally, and spiritually. I feel like Humpty Dumpty. I fell off the wall, cracked in a million pieces and now all the King's men are trying to put me back together again. Good thing my King happens to be not only the King of Kings but also the Lord of Lords.

At one point in my cancer journey, I stood before the mirror, bald and breastless. I didn't recognize myself. A/C Chemotherapy shoots all the hair out of the body. Within fourteen days I was bald . . . everywhere. A double mastectomy leaves a woman completely breastless, like a blank wall, breast tissue, nipples and all. As a teenager, I was told I resembled Brook Shields. As I hit my twenties and thirties, it had been a split between Julia Roberts and Sandra Bullock. However, as I stood looking at myself in the mirror I now resembled something from *Star Wars*. I felt androgynous. The tears and wailing that came out of this experience still resonate throughout my soul. I remember screaming out to God, "What!? What else do you want from me? I have nothing left!" It was at this low moment that something silenced me. I stood in disbelief as I surveyed the damage.

The realization hit me. I was thirty-eight years old and I have cancer. How was this possible? My great grandmother lived into her nineties; my grandfather was ninety-three. There is no breast cancer in my family to speak of. I even got tested for the gene, which I didn't have. How? Why? I'm in excellent health. I'm a personal trainer in martial arts. I have my second-degree black belt in Tae Kwon Do. I barely drink, I don't smoke, I eat six small meals a day, I avoid sugar, I take vitamins, and I exercise daily. I also pray every day; most days, I pray throughout the entire day—on and off. I have learned that it's not about *what I do* in life it's about *who I am* in life in relation to love—love of God, others and myself.

As I stood in a silent stupor of disbelief, a verse from the Bible came to my mind, it was a verse that I had preached since I was seventeen years old to youth groups for the past twenty years. I had a radical faith conversion that I experienced at seventeen when I fell in love with Jesus and His message of love, life and freedom. The verse... yes, this verse came to my mind yet in a profoundly different way than ever before. Before, I would preach this verse with authority, as if quoting it from some famous author. Now, however, I wasn't preaching it, I was living it out: *"The Lord does not look at the things man looks at. Man looks at the outward appearance, but the Lord looks at the heart"* (1 Samuel 16:7). Man/woman looks at what he/she sees with his/her eyes... God sees man/woman from the heart. He sees us from the inside out, not the outside in. Someone once told me that God doesn't even see our physical bodies; he only sees our soul. This verse came to me at one of the lowest points in my battle, I believe, to save my life. For it was at this moment in time that the true essence of my whole existence here on earth was revealed to me. Being completely stripped of everything physically that I had attached a large portion of my identity to as a woman, ultimately ended up setting me free. It became very clear to me in this vulnerable state of *being* that my purpose was to learn how to see myself as I truly am, to love myself right where I am, and then offer the same grace to others.

I am here to look at my heart, not my outer appearance, to find my true, authentic self. I am here to learn how to love God, others, and myself *from my heart* and to see God, others, and myself *from the heart,* not from outer rituals, appearances, or accomplishments.

I think it's important for me to reveal to you a bit of my past in order for you to understand where I am coming from in my conversations with Jesus. I grew up in an upper-middle class family on Long Island, New York. I am the second oldest of four siblings—two brothers and one sister. I love my family deeply. I basically had a dream childhood—no divorce, no cancer, no real tragedy to speak of, until I was seventeen; ironically it was the same year that my personal faith in God kicked in.

I fell in love with a guy (John) at seventeen, a true soul mate. we connected on every level. In fact, I attribute the beginning of my faith walk to his presence in my life. Before I was seventeen, I was a wild woman, living for the moment—yet in a destructive way, drinking, smoking pot, messing around a ton, and lying all the time about what I was doing. Then I met John . . . the first time I saw him, he was saying a quiet prayer over his meal. This was a man who said, "If it weren't for my relationship with God, I would rise and fall depending on how the world judged me at that time." That statement haunted my soul so profoundly that it changed my entire outlook on life and who and what I was living for. It started the journey inside of me, raising my awareness of love and the source of love. We shared this spiritual bond, which I had never experienced before in a relationship. It was based on the connection of our hearts to, with, and in divine love rather than just physical love.

John was planning on moving out to Colorado when I went to college in Boulder. Everything seemed perfect. Almost one year into our relationship, he was killed in a car accident. I still remember what I was wearing when his sister called me. "Lauren, there has been a terrible car accident . . . John was in it."

The pause on the phone seemed like eternity. I remember wondering if I even wanted to ask the next question, and before I could filter it, the words came tumbling out of my mouth. "Is he okay? Where is he? What hospital is he at?"

Silence . . . a silence I will never forget. In that silence, everything inside my body began to scream against what I knew I would hear next. "Lauren, he was killed instantly." That moment is seared on my heart forever. The next thing I remember, I was running out my door. I ran for as long as my lungs held out, screaming, crying out against the whole reality of death; I was weeping from a place I never knew existed inside of me. At night, I would stay awake and stare into the dark for hours, asking God if I could see his face one more time, hear his voice, kiss his face. I remember having a choice to continue to hope and trust in God's plan for my life or stay in a state of angry paralysis over the fact that I that I lost my potential soul mate . . . I chose God. I still think of him and feel his presence very profoundly during moments of suffering.

That was my first real encounter with death—death of someone I truly loved—but not the last. After John's death, I lost three friends to cancer . . . all my age. I think that there are two kinds of people in life: those who are overcome and those *who overcome.* Again I had a choice . . . I am learning that I always have a choice. I can't help what happens in my life when it comes to life and death but I can always choose how I respond to it. I chose hope and trust once again. I can't help but think that I was being prepared for the trial of cancer that I am currently walking through now.

I got married at twenty-one to a man I met in college. we dated eleven months before we were engaged. I entered marriage still carrying the deep loss and longing for what I shared with John. I was married two weeks after I graduated college. We had a huge "Great Gatsby" wedding reception on the water. I believe in marriage, and I have had an incredible example of marriage in my parent's relationship. Mine did not work out. I am the only divorced person in my entire family. I was married for seventeen years. In the first few years of our marriage, I started to sense that something was wrong. I began to realize how vastly different our core needs were, yet because of my strong belief in marriage, I was determined to make it work. I have a very strong German work ethic that is woven into my being. I was told during this past year that I honored the sacred vow over my own heart. Looking back, I see clearly that I was the walking wounded entering into my marriage. I chose a man who could not and did not want to enter into the relationship beyond a certain point. At that time, it was very safe for me because subconsciously I was protecting myself from the potential emotional, spiritual loss that I experienced with John's death. My ex-husband is a wonderful person, and I believe that the reason we have been able to remain friends through this whole divorce is because we have respect for each other. We have learned to love and accept each other for who we are along with a deep understanding that we did not have the essential ingredients needed for an intimate marriage relationship. The annulment was granted to us within a few months.

However, the pain and rejection that I experienced trying to make my marriage work slowly ate away at me throughout the years. I often felt as if I was trying to squeeze orange juice from a banana; it was not going to happen. The more I tried to create deeper connection with my husband, the further away I pushed him, and that pattern started early on in the marriage. I felt as if I experienced an emotional divorce long before anything ever surfaced. In fact, one year before I found out I had cancer, I wrote in my journal that I felt like I was slowly dying inside . . . and I was. I tried various things throughout the years in an attempt to distract myself from my feelings of rejection . . . I joined different religious groups and became very active in Tae Kwon Do, looking for physical affirmation. At one point, I actually looked into becoming a Nun in an attempt to make sense of the lack of intimacy in my marriage. I was desperately seeking identity and validation in the midst of intense feelings of rejection.

My three beautiful children are the greatest gifts to me from my marriage. Now that I have been thrown into early menopause because of the treatments, the depth of my gratitude for my children is tenfold!

That is a brief summary of my life to date . . . *a very brief one.* I have always prayed, yet I began to write down very specific responses that started to come to me very clearly over the past five years. I am not a saint . . . I am not anything more or less than who I truly am, a wounded soldier who has recently emerged victoriously from a horrific battle in life—for life. It has been through my wounds and brokenness that I have gained a profound awareness into the purpose of my life and the essence of who I truly am through God's eyes. I am still in treatment as well as reconstruction. There are no guarantees that this cancer will not come back. Every day before I put my feet on the ground, I pause to connect with the one who holds every heartbeat in the palm of his hand. I thank God for my breath and another day of life—everything else after that is simply icing on my cake! I truly believe that all things work together in my life for an ultimate good, and when that good reaches completion, I hear Jesus' voice saying, "It is finished." I came out of my divorce with many wounds—low self-esteem, deep feelings of rejections, and a sense of failure. I questioned whether or not I was truly capable of being loved and loving from a sense of wholeness rather than from the insecure feelings that accompany neediness. Through the experience of suffering, God revealed, and continues to reveal, to me the truth of who I am as well as how loved I am from the inside out—by God, others and most importantly by myself. I've learned that I cannot give what I don't have. As Jesus says,

"Ask and it will be given to you; seek and you will find; knock and the door shall be opened to you" (Matthew 7:7).

"Give and it will be given to you. A good measure, pressed down, shaken together and running over, will be poured into your lap" (Luke 6:38).

As I was lying on the floor wailing after my cancer diagnosis, I remember crying out between sobs to God, "I can't handle this . . . I can't do this . . . this is too much . . . if you want me to live, you have to carry me to where you want me to be . . . carry me." God used the hands and hearts of hundreds of people to carry me back to the place of wholeness and love that I had lost within myself over the years. He restored my joy through the darkest valley that I have ever walked through in my life.

I had tremendous guilt that accompanied my separation and divorce. I was plagued with this question: "Did I do enough . . . did I do everything in my power to save this marriage?" In many of the journal entries, I am working through this guilt toward a place of understanding. I've learned that guilt paralyzes me . . . awareness, forgiveness and most profoundly *love* motivate and inspire me to ask myself, *What is it that I am supposed to learn from this experience? In what areas can I grow closer to God, others and myself through this? Who am I? Where am I here? And what will it matter?* I've also experienced the profound truth revealed in the following verse:

"Above all else, guard your heart, for it is the wellspring of life" (Proverbs 4:23).

Every morning I wake up and pray, "Thank you God for another day of life! Help me to learn how to love better today." It has been made very clear to me that love is the answer to suffering. As suffering has increased in my life, love all the more—to the point that the suffering has become a vehicle for more love. I have full confidence that with every storm Jesus comes too. Yes, suffering is a means by which the human heart is expanded in such a way that more love can enter in and therefore, more love flows out. I have such faith in this cycle that fear has been pushed aside and love and confidence have replaced it. Truly, there is no room for fear in the heart that is consumed by love. This love I speak of, that I have encountered throughout my life, flows from the source of all love—divine love. God is instructing my heart in the way of divine love, a love that is reckless, daring and profoundly self-aware in all situations.

You will often hear three voices as you read through each entry: the scripture, Jesus, and mine. Read with an open heart. It is my prayer that you will grow in your awareness of how loved you are right where you are at as well as in your desire to know yourself, God, and others freely and authentically. This is a glimpse into my journey toward life and internal freedom. May the following conversations with Jesus inspire you to embrace and authentically live out your own journey of life. You can read each entry as a daily devotional sequentially or randomly. Each entry contains its own message, just as each soul contains its own journey.

• • •

Enjoy two *Edge God In Podcast* Previews designed to "Champion Your Human Potential in Christ." *See how at the end of this book.*

Edge God In Foundational Scriptures:
1. "Be transformed by the renewing of your mind" (Romans 12:1).
2. "It is for freedom that Christ has set us free. Stand firm, then, and do not allow yourselves to be burdened again by the yoke of slavery" (Galatians 5:1).

Edge God In Mission Statement:

Our mission is to "Edge God In" by championing human potential in and through Christ as we integrate sacred scripture into our words, thoughts, deeds, and actions. Edge God In programs are Christian programs that empower God's people with specific skill sets and techniques that teach the "how-to" needed to make Romans 12:1 and Galatians 5:1 a sustainable reality in our day to day walk with God, personally and professionally. Using podcasts, virtual Bible studies, retreats, seminars, life coaching, interactive workshops, speaking events and trainings, our programs are designed to equip youth and adults with a backpack filled with grab and go tools to help renew our mind in Christ and release the yoke of slavery in the midst of a world that Edges God Out (EGO) with shiny objects.

BEFORE

DECEMBER 5, 2000

"I tell you the truth, anyone who will not receive the kingdom of God like a little child will never enter it" (Mark 10:15).

Me: Teach me wisdom that comes from being a child.

Jesus: Indulge yourself in the moment my child . . . for it is in the moment that you will encounter love most profoundly. Consider the play of a child . . . he experiences the moment without any thought to how others perceive him . . . he moves from the truth in his heart, and he has no fear about living out that truth moment to moment. He moves freely with full confidence that he is loved unconditionally deep within his soul . . . this awareness of my limitless love drives out all fears. Children are natural contemplatives and they live in the freedom of my love . . . as do you . . . yet too often, you let this truth slip out of your mind. Contemplate me and you will not be able to resist being present to my love . . . I tell you, this will free you from all your worldly burdens that have become a yoke of slavery for you in your life. Contemplate love without any conditions or boundaries. Love for the sake of love alone. When you contemplate me, you contemplate love . . . in this lies your freedom. Allow my limitless love to swallow up your limitedness . . . come, my child, be present to the one who is the great I AM . . . trust that I will carry you to the place you are meant to be.

MARCH 6, 2001

"Are you so foolish? After beginning with the Spirit, are you now trying to attain your goal by human effort?" (Galatians 3:3).

Me: My self-esteem is based too much on the outcome of what I do in my life. Knowing that I feel good when I have a sense of control over people and events in my life keeps me chained to a cycle of discontent . . . I continue to lose control every day. Show me the truth that comes from knowing that when I let go of control I am still okay . . . even more so!

Jesus: My child, you get so frustrated so quickly when you continue to fall. You focus on control over people and events. If you only knew how much I desire to carry what burdens your heart. What frustrates you again and again is the fact that you have no control. It is a lie to think you will ever have control over any event, person, or situation. Again, your frustration comes from thinking you will gain control. The only thing I have allowed you to have control over is how you respond to different people and events in your life . . . you can always choose between fear and love. Remember, my child, apart from love, you can do nothing of any lasting value. Surrender, my little wild flower, move all of your faculties toward this one goal: surrender. Allow grace to carry you through every event and remember my promises. You can do all things through me; my yoke is easy and my burden is light, I give peace to your soul that the world cannot offer, this is because the world will always choose what is against me. You are not of the world; step out and be separate from the world. Remember the world and its desires will pass away, but the one who does the will of God shall live forever. His will is that you surrender all that you are to love and that you trust with all of your heart that I will care for you with the tenderness of unconditional love. I will see you through all situations in this way when you abide in me. Be present to me as a child is present to life. Remember I AM, the great I AM and you will encounter love most intimately when you remain in the moment.

You have not because you ask not, ask and you will receive all that your heart and soul truly hunger and thirst for. Yes, you are discouraged by your lack of faith and your inability to let go and trust when life is so full of challenges and trials. But I encourage you once again to surrender all of these feelings to love. Do this moment by moment in your day and you will feel contentment. Allow the fire of my love to burn away any doubts, fears, and anxieties. Pray that only one desire will emerge from the flames and that is the desire to love. So great a love I desire for you that you will remain untouched by the events, people, and situations of the world that used to trouble your mind and leave your heart unsettled. When you set your heart as a seal upon mine, you will know such a complete love and will have everything you need for life and Godliness. Knowing this will set you free and the people, experiences, and situations that once troubled your soul will now brush by you with little to no effect upon you.

Love and surrender lead to true freedom. Seek it with all of your heart, mind, soul, and strength. You will dance and sing with joy. Then go forth and love the souls I put in your life without expectation of being loved in return. This is a pilgrim's love. Remember, you are just passing through this world, you belong to me, I paid a high price to have you, and your purpose I have made very clear: Love one another as I have loved you. My gift was free so also yours must be. Remain in me and I will remain in you always. My love for you is more than you can bear; it is truly all consuming. Set your hearts on things above.

May 20, 2001

"All the people saw this and began to mutter, "He has gone to be the guest of a 'sinner.' But Zacchaeus stood up and said to the Lord, 'Look, Lord! Here and now I give half of my possessions to the poor, and if I have cheated anybody out of anything, I will pay back four times the amount.' Jesus said to him, 'Today salvation has come to this house" (Luke 19:8–9).

Me: I used to think that I knew the perfect way to get to you, Lord. I found myself judging others if they went another way. I am starting to see that every human being has something to teach me . . . each soul reveals new insight into you and me. Show me how to touch every soul with love.

Jesus: You cannot force yourself into the human heart. The hearts of my children are won over through unconditional love that is patiently poured out over time into their souls. To do this, you must first enter into their experiences . . . what moves their heart, no matter how worldly it may seem to eyes that have been enlightened to heavenly things. In order to win the confidence of man's heart, you must first step into his world. Then you earn the right to speak the truth in love and he will listen because you have loved him where he is without judgment. Your love for them will increase within their heart the desire to do what is right in God's eyes. Because God is love, he moves souls into his heart through love alone. Take Zacchaeus for example, one soul living in sin . . . I went to his house, ate his food at his table with his friends. I entered into his life experience with great love and acceptance. My love entering into his life exposed the dark deeds of his soul thereby leading him to repentance and reconciliation. You must do the same to win hearts for me.

It is pride and ego that keep you from stepping into the lives of those who are entranced by the things of the world. Rather than expending energy on worrying about how you don't fit into the world and how people cannot relate to the depth of intimacy we share together . . . step away from yourself and enter into the lives of those who misunderstand and persecute you. Are you not my own little ambassador of love? Only through intense love will they begin to understand your source of joy. Do I not enter into your worldly experiences? Is it not my great love and mercy in spite of your acts of disobedience that continue to draw your heart into mine? Do the same for one another. Love first, then lead. Follow my example . . . meet everyone on the road just as the Father ran to meet the prodigal son. Go and meet others, love them, take time to listen, and experience their joys and sorrows . . . all with great love and mercy and in time you will earn the right to speak the truth in love. Through love and mercy their eyes will be opened to the condition of their soul . . . just as yours is. Do not forget the depths from which you were saved so that pride will not draw you away from my love. It is the desire that I see . . . the desire always over the actions . . . offer the same grace to the souls around you . . . see others for what they desire to be apart from all the pain that causes them to act out . . . just as I continue to see you.

SEPTEMBER 22, 2001

"But many who are first will be last, and many who are last will be first" (Matthew 19:30).

Me: What should I do Lord? I care too much about what people think of me. Please tell me how I can train my flesh to seek you first above all other comforts in this world . . . I am weak, and I grow weary at times so quickly looking for you amidst my circumstances. I fall too quickly. I often fall because I don't want to suffer, so I look for quick hits in the flesh to keep me going. Please help me love you better. Show me how to stay small Lord . . . so there is more room for you to fill me up with your largeness!

Jesus: Ofttimes you search for comfort for the cravings of your flesh . . . which often revolve around your desire to be accepted and approved by others. You look for ways to free your flesh from the discomfort of hungering for approval from those you love when all the while the answers to your cravings, my small child, are found within my love for you. When your soul encounters even a grain of my love, it begins to bloom wherever it is planted. The results always lead to a sense of wholeness.

    Has there ever been a time when I have not met you when you have turned to me with a sincere heart desiring my love? I know my sheep and my sheep know me, they recognize my voice and no one shall snatch them out of my hands. Believe in my words, for in them the treasures of the Kingdom of God are found. You often ask me for a mind filled with wisdom and revelation so that you may know me better. I encourage you to continue to make the time to receive all the riches of wisdom that I freely pour into your small heart. I will be found by all who seek me.

You ask about remaining small . . . this too is a choice involving desire and will. When you have the desire first, it is much easier to conform the will to that desire with my grace . . . as you know from the Scriptures, apart from me you can do nothing. Desire to be small, let that take root in all you do . . . think in every moment, How can I be smaller for you, Jesus? I was the smallest; I know how to help you in this area because I took on the form of the smallest, weakest man—an infant—totally dependent on my mother for life. My sweet mother gave me the care I needed in one of my weakest moments physically speaking in my life on earth, next to the cross. I started my journey small and I ended my journey small. As an infant, I was totally dependent on my parents for life. As a man of sorrows, many sorrows on the cross, I was very small . . . without a home, without friends, without all of the comforts that the world offers. I remained small yet remember, it was because of my small, humble, broken state that the glory of my Father and his power to offer salvation to the world was able to be accomplished through me. It is the same for you my little child . . . the smaller and more broken you become, the more profoundly you will experience the power of my Father's love and mercy.

Take captive each thought and moment for this one goal: humility (smallness), love and confidence in my ability to carry you into all of these. *Do not be afraid to suffer!* Suffering is the natural process of fear and weakness leaving the soul only to reveal more strength, hope and courage needed to live life to the fullest. Pray that the hardness of hearts will be dissolved through my love. Every soul fears that they will not be able to survive the experiences of the world; I say that I have already overcome all of your fears, all of the anxieties that keep you in a state of paralysis . . . I have overcome them all with love. You have that same strength within you. The same strength to overcome the fears and anxieties that hold you in bondage . . . you have been set free; there is no battle between fear and love . . . love always wins out . . . embrace this truth! Know that all events in life are sent for the purpose of growth and learning . . . learning to love more completely and learning how to allow yourself to be loved more completely . . . learning the essence of forgiveness of oneself and others . . . truly I say to you embrace these truths for they are the pathway to your freedom, the great exodus for your enslaved soul. Embrace, surrender to, and live with confidence in the truth that nothing will happen in your life that you will not be able to overcome with love and forgiveness. For even death itself is swallowed up in the victory of this truth. Perfect love truly casts out all fears.

Me: Lord, I desire to live in the freedom of your love and forgiveness. Give me enough love for myself so that I will have the courage to forgive myself, and in return for that self-forgiveness, I will then have the strength within to forgive those who have acted out their pain on me in my life. I will then be free. Free to love and be loved . . . to know and to be known. As you love and know me.

March 7, 2002

"Do not love the world or anything in the world. If anyone loves the world, the love of the Father is not in him. For everything in the world—the cravings of sinful man, the lust of his eyes and the boasting of what he has and does—comes not from the Father but from the world. The world and its desires pass away, but the man who does the will of God lives forever" (1 John 2:15–17).

Me: Lord, when I resist indulging in what I desire to possess in this world, I find myself in a position to offer you some small gift of self-denial and death to self, making more room for authentic love. When I am given the opportunity to offer up the things that I want, the things that bring me immediate satisfaction and pleasure, I enter more profoundly into the freedom that you died to give me. I am no longer a slave to that which I experience through my senses; rather I become captivated by the things that truly satisfy the cravings of my soul. The riches of heaven that flow from your most sacred heart swallow up the emptiness, and I am truly satisfied once again! When I surrender to you any desire or need I may have in my flesh, it is then that I realize that you alone satisfy the deepest longings of my soul. Everything can be summed up in one statement, "Love must be the goal behind every action, every thought . . . love behind me, before me, within me. . . . Everything done for the sake of love leads my soul into the experience of heaven on earth. From your heart flows all of the comforts my soul seeks in this world. Have your way with me, Lord; in spite of myself . . . your way is always the way of love. May my fears and pride never prevent your love and grace from using my soul to draw another into love. Set me free from all fear that comes from not believing that I am completely loved and accepted just as I am in your eyes! Believing this truth will set me free from the opinions of the world that so often hold me captive . . . what should it matter if the whole world should come against me if my heart is right with you?

Jesus: When you get out of your own way, the way of love floods in and all around you. Everything unfolds perfectly like a beautiful rose without any effort on your part. For this is love's nature. Love evokes more love and your joy is complete . . . heaven on earth.

MARCH 25, 2002

"Give me wisdom and knowledge, that I may lead this people, for who is able to govern this great people of yours?' God said to Solomon, "Since this is your heart's desire and you have not asked for wealth, riches or honor, nor for the death of your enemies, and since you have not asked for a long life but for wisdom and knowledge to govern my people over whom I have made you king, therefore wisdom and knowledge will be given you. And I will also give you wealth, riches and honor, such as no king who was before you ever had and none after you will have" (2 Chronicles 1:11–12).

Jesus: What do you want from me?

Me: I want to see your beautiful face, put my hand on your cheek. I want to kiss your loving hands . . . the same hands that healed the sick and comforted the grieving. I want to see your feet, hold them in my hands, and wash them with my tears. I want to lay my head on your chest and hear the beat of your heart . . . listen to the flow of your blood, the same blood that feeds my body, that connects me to your heart, your desires, and your will.

Jesus, sweet Jesus, you are *everything* to me. Without love, I am nothing. You are the embodiment of love and you embody me. Set me free Lord from all of the sin that so easily entangles me so that I can run the race with endurance. "I am alone," I say at times yet, this is not true for you surround me each second of the day! I am never alone; I am always in you . . . always! Help me to stay close to your side . . . to see you, hear you, and lose myself in your passion this week more than ever before.

I am still in the Garden of Gethsemane with you . . . for I am paralyzed by what I see and feel. Help me move beyond the garden, into your passion, all the way to the cross. Give me the courage and come lead me to you so that I will never be the same again. I want to go with you . . . please take me so that your will and work may be accomplished more completely through my incomplete soul, for it is only by witnessing your anguish, pain, fear, and triumph over death, that I am able to be love and mercy to those you thirst for . . . those you died for . . . those you love without conditions.

Jesus: You are never the same. When you walk in the way of love, you are constantly evolving into deeper realms of love's expression within your soul. Your soul is and always has been complete, not lacking anything for true life, love, and godliness. My work is accomplished perfectly just as is evident in the beautiful nature that surrounds you . . . no need for anxiety, fear or doubt, only a gentle resolve to surrender to the process of love and life made manifest through form. Surrender my child, for this is your entrance into internal freedom.

SEPTEMBER 24, 2002

"He who has an ear, let him hear what the Spirit says to the churches. To him who overcomes, I will give the right to eat from the tree of life, which is the paradise of God" (Revelation 1:7).

Me: Jesus, I want to be a joy to you! I desire with all my heart, Lord, to be a little flower of your love and mercy in the midst of this world unto my death! Help me, Jesus, to see clearly; as you know, Lord, I am blind . . . touch my eyes so that I can see and my ears so that I can hear! I am a very physical person, and I get so much of my sense of identity from what I see, feel, hear, and touch . . . I desire to move beyond this focus knowing that when I get what my flesh desires, it is fleeting.

Jesus: I love you from a place that is free from the confinements of your five senses. When you made the decision to find me, you allowed yourself to be loved by me. You see, I love all my children in this way, yet many do not choose to receive the love I constantly offer them. Many as you know live as enemies of my cross. Remember the Scriptures you claim to love and believe them with all of your heart so that you will not doubt that you are a joy to me. "I stand at the door and knock. If anyone hears my voice and opens the door I will come in and eat with him, and he with me" (Revelation 3:20). You see, my little flower, I am eating with you, and you are feeding on my very life and love. Two things only do I require of my children. First, that they hear my voice calling out to them, beckoning them, desiring them to listen to me, hear me, love me in them . . . too many ears are made deaf by the clamor of the world. The evil one desires that all ears would remain in a state of deafness to my voice, allowing them to be consumed with satisfying the flesh, knowing that the slightest awareness of the smallest whisper would begin to cure them of their deafness and lead them into true life. The ears must open first before the eyes begin to see the sacredness of life that surrounds each soul.

Me: You flood my soul with love!

Jesus: Yes, my sweet, small flower . . . I know what floods your soul . . . for it is I that am the source of all that moves you at this moment . . . be still and listen to what I speak to your heart for it is not for you alone. No, these words are life and truth for all of my children. Remember who you are in me . . . you are a fragrant offering of love and mercy. I am the source of all fragrance for abundant life, love, and mercy . . . you are a little flower that I am using to flood the world around you with my sweet fragrance of love and mercy. Do not hold it back! Stay small, my little child; the smaller you are the greater my fragrance through your life will be.

I must continue to speak to you about the two things that I require of my children. The first I have told you is to hear my voice; the second one is to open the door of their heart as a sign of inviting me into fellowship with them. After these two gestures of desire occur, is there anything that I will withhold from them? No, everything they need for life and godliness is theirs! For once I am eating with my children at the table of love, the secrets of the Kingdom of God will be shared. I desire that all my children hear my voice and open the door of their hearts to love. My Father's love is so great that he gave it without cost. Opening the door and hearing my voice is as simple as taking your next breath.

Me: Then why wouldn't every soul choose this?

Jesus: Because of the nature to sin. To turn away from my Father and to seek selfish gain and pursue self-interests all lead to deafness and the inability to hear me calling their names. I assure you that I do not cease to call out the names of my children; my calling and beckoning never cease to occur. Pray constantly for my voice of love to be heard unto the ends of the world. Remember the snake that Moses lifted up in the desert to save the children? My Father's heart was beckoning as it always is for his children to turn and look upon the snake to be healed. Listen carefully . . . I am truly the one through which any soul who looks upon me, who hears me, and opens the door to me, will be saved. Pray for a change of heart. Rebuke the noise of sin that deafens the ears and prevents the soul from entering into the freedom of love.

September 25, 2002

"But godliness with contentment is great gain. For we brought nothing into the world, and we can take nothing out of it" (1 Timothy 6:6).

Me: Attachments and expectations continue to chain me down to this world . . .

Jesus: Have no expectation other than to be loved by me. Expect this of me my child, for I am love, and I exist for the very purpose of filling the hearts of my children with my love. Expect this of me. This is confidence that leads to freedom from dependency on the world. The world offers you immediate satisfactions with results that are fleeting. This is why you continue to hunger and thirst for more. When you set your heart after the momentary appeasements of the world, you set yourself up for the vicious cycle of discontentment. Oh, yes, you will receive a momentary rush of pleasure, yet it is quickly swallowed up by your cravings for more of that which you do not need . . . more poison that seduces the senses into wanting, envying and coveting . . . to what avail? Truly, truly, I say to you these things will perish even as you grab a hold of them, leaving you empty and wallowing in discontentment.

The verse you constantly seek after, "Godliness with contentment is great gain," is truly a treasure from the wisdom from within my heart (1 Timothy 6:6). Godliness is love. God is love. The Heavenly Father desires that all his children live within his love—free from desire and want, free from all jealousies and fears. All such anxieties stem from the cravings of the flesh. It is very simple. Contentment can only flow from the creator into the creation. The creation is only content when it feels the hand of its creator guiding its movements through life.

Me: How can this be, Lord?

Jesus: Remain in Me. The Father and I are one. No matter how loud the world becomes around you, step into union with me in the quiet of your heart, so that you can experience godliness and contentment because you are united in purpose with your creator, who is love. Love will set you free! Stay with me within the moments of your days; stay with me and bear the fruit of contentment. Surrender to these truths and trust that I will act. Forget yourself, and you will find contentment and peace. Be still and listen. Empty yourself of all that you have attached yourself to in this world . . . the emptier you become, the greater opportunity you will have to be filled with even more love!

SEPTEMBER 27, 2002

"Lazarus is dead, and for your sake I am glad I was not there, so that you may believe . . ." your brother will rise again." Martha answered, "I know he will rise again in the resurrection at the last day." Jesus said to her, "I am the resurrection and the life. He who believes in me will live, even though he dies; and whoever lives and believes in me will never die. Do you believe this?" . . ." Where have you laid him?" he asked. "Come and see, Lord," they replied. Jesus wept" (John 11:14–15, 22–26, 34–35).

Me: What was behind your tears, my sweet Jesus? Speak, Lord, your child is listening.

Jesus: I was a man of many sorrows, my little flower, many sorrows. My hunger and thirst for souls to put full confidence in my love and mercy continues to consume my heart's longings. At the time when my beloved friend Mary approached me, my heart was once again filled with sorrow due to the fact that I see the weakness within the human heart to trust in my Father and me. The weakness within the human heart to abandon themselves in confidence to my Father's perfect will knowing that his all-consuming love devours all doubts, fears and sorrows, is endless. My sorrow comes from the depths of my heart's longing to free my children from this fear of death, for in me, there is only life. When I was approached by my children weeping over Lazarus's death, I wept over the death of perfect union that we once shared in the garden together. I wept over the hardening of your hearts. I wept over the choices you make to continually rely more on the world for your peace, comfort, and wisdom rather than turning to my Father and me through whom all wisdom, love, and mercy flow.

Listen, my child: when you know you have the perfect gift to give to the one you love and he continually goes elsewhere looking for that perfect gift, your sorrow is great! You are continually denied the opportunity to know that your beloved prefers you to the things that not only harm your beloved but also result in death. Yes, I am a man of many sorrows yet with one desire: that all souls would turn from the grief of death and all roads that lead to death, and look upon me to be healed and restored to life . . . having great faith that I will not deny them in their hunger and thirst for love and inner peace.

This was my desire at the time of Lazarus' death, and this is my desire for all eternity: that all will come and eat with me . . . longing to be one with my Father and me . . . that their joy would be complete in our union. My tears fall easily over this passion of mine . . . make it your own. Everything I share, my child, is and always has been for love, by love for the purpose of teaching the truth that all that you truly desire in life flows from your hunger to know that you are loved just as you are . . . allow love to be your guide in all you do and your joy will be complete.

SEPTEMBER 28, 2002

"Brothers, we do not want you to be ignorant about those who fall asleep, or to grieve like the rest of men, who have no hope. We believe that Jesus died and rose again and so we believe that God will bring with Jesus those who have fallen asleep in him" (1 Thessalonians 4:13–14).

Me: My sweet savior, I adore you with all my being! Forgive me for any moments that I do not remain undivided in my affections toward you. Last night, I was sad; I lost a family member I love very deeply. I felt you very close to me . . . I experienced a rocking of my body as if you were embracing me and rocking me in your arms. My joy was overwhelming . . . through my tears the light of hope radiated throughout my being . . . speak to me about this encounter please . . .

Jesus: My sweet little flower, you continually seek union with me, and in every way, I surround you with my love . . . you run to embrace all you can get! This is a joy to your sweet savior, as you call me, my love for you is sweet and it envelops your entire being. Yes, you felt a rocking movement that guided you through the worship music that surrounded you. That was my embrace . . . I know your sadness over your temporal loss; I remind you that it is only temporal. She lives in my embrace now . . . free from all fears, worries, and anxieties. She is constantly enraptured by her beloved savior . . . her love and concern for you have remained untouched by the first death; she has experienced the completion of her love for you, and her care and concern for you now have eternal value and meaning. Let your tears flow my child, yet allow them to be used for others who suffer, doubt, and live in a state of hopelessness. Allow your tears to include all who live in a constant state of fear and loneliness. Allow them to flow for the sake of all hearts that have grown cold to my voice, who have chosen the darkness and emptiness of the world over the light and life in their savior. For all those who do not know that death is simply taking off your cloak of mortality and putting on your cloak of immortality, of experiencing completely the truth of eternal love that is limitless. Death is always swallowed up by the victory of my relentless love . . . I overcame it for your sake to prove the reality of this truth . . . there is no room for fear. You are surrounded, continually by those who you love that have gone before you . . . you exhale one last breath from this limited world only to inhale your next breath in the limitless reality of eternity . . . where death is swallowed up in the victory of my love. Remember this. Share with the world the comfort that flows within your soul from knowing these truths.

SEPTEMBER 29, 2002

"But if you suffer for doing good and you endure it, this is commendable before God. To this you were called, because Christ suffered for you, leaving you an example, that you should follow in his step. 'He committed no sin, and no deceit was found in his mouth.' When they hurled their insults at him, he did not retaliate; when he suffered, he made no threats. Instead, he entrusted himself to him who judges justly. He himself bore our sins in his body on the tree, so that we might die to sins and live for righteousness; by his wounds you have been healed. For you were like sheep going astray, but now you have returned to the Shepherd and Overseer of your souls" (1 Peter 2:23–25).

Me: Jesus, I desire to catch in my heart all of the mercies and love that continually flow from your heart so that they do not fall to the earth unnoticed. Please give me this honor!

Jesus: You have this honor, my sweet little flower, for you have only to express a small desire to receive such a privilege due to your hearts longing for me for the sake of all who pass me by without so much as a glance. Yes, I am the poor beggar, the one that is avoided and rejected by all who pass by . . . yet I will not cease to look for any gesture of curiosity or desire . . . just a glance, a pause, a thought, a step toward my homeless existence. This is all it takes for me to enter in and begin my work of salvation in the human heart. That is my quest . . . I am a homeless man looking for a home and how beautiful will my home be in the hearts of the broken and lonely. For they turn over all the keys to their heart to me much more quickly than those who are satiated by the world. Be small and broken my little one, give to me all keys

. . . I am a homeless beggar . . . I never cease in begging to find a home in the hearts of my children.

Me: Take all keys, Lord! My whole being longs to have you as the master of this household . . . make me beautiful for you; I beg you. I am homeless without you, Jesus!

Jesus: All of my children are beautiful . . . due to insecurities; they are blinded from recognizing this truth. Come let us build a home together! Its beauty will be unmatched by anything the world has to offer. Everything built together will last beyond this earthly experience into all of eternity. Hold onto my hand that was pierced out of love for you. Remember, my child, on earth, I was a carpenter, and I still am . . . always creating beautiful masterpieces out of the most unlikely materials.

OCTOBER 4, 2002

"So we make it our goal to please him, whether we are at home in the body or away from it. For we must all appear before the judgment seat of Christ, that each one may receive what is due him for the things done while in the body, whether good or bad" (2 Corinthians 5:9–10).

Me: Oh, that my soul would become a perfect place for you to dwell and accomplish your most perfect will through! I asked you today to draw my heart into your sufferings . . . particularly during your passion. You blessed me with a vision of the docile slain lamb wounded yet still receiving scourging without the slightest effort to move away from it. Again, you came to me when I asked about how we will feel about all of the sin we have committed during our lives when we come before you. You said we will feel just the way Isaiah, Paul, and Peter felt when they recognized you.

"Woe to me!" I cried. "I am ruined! For I am a man of unclean lips, and I live among a people of unclean lips, and my eyes have seen the king. The Lord Almighty" (Isaiah 6:5).

"When Simeon Peter saw this, he fell at Jesus' knees and said, 'Go away from me, Lord; I am a sinful man!'" (Luke 5:8).

"For I am the least of the apostles and do not even deserve to be called an apostle, because I persecuted the Church of God" (1 Corinthians 14:9).

We will be painfully aware of our fallen state; our soul will grieve deeply over every unkind word spoken and over every unkind act that offended and wounded another soul.

Your very presence will burn through our being, revealing all of our thoughts and actions, refining us into your love. This will be a cleansing of the soul that will bring much discomfort, yet it will ultimately set us free from our wounds. Lord, help me to remember that your response to our fallen condition is *love*. It has always been and will continue to be so throughout all eternity. Love knows and understands that any unkind word or deed flows out of the reservoir of our own pain acted out. It is a love that purifies, cleanses, and renews. A love that restores in an instant that which has been broken and misused. You did this countless times throughout history . . . the thief on the cross being one of the most profound examples of what you do with a desire for you in spite of sin. Your words of reconciliation and renewed hope spoken to Isaiah, Peter, and Paul, three souls who could barely stand to be in your presence, give strength to my soul.

"Then one of the seraphs flew to me with a live coal in his hand, which he had taken with tongs from the altar. With it he touched my mouth and said, 'See, this has touched your lips; your guilt is taken away and your sin atoned for.' Then I heard the voice of the Lord saying, 'Whom shall I send? And who will go for us?' And I said, 'Here am I. Send me!'" (Isaiah 6:6–8).

"Then Jesus said to Simon, 'Don't be afraid; from now on you will catch men." (Luke 5:10).

"Go! This man (Paul) is my chosen instrument to carry my name before the Gentiles and their kings and before the people of Israel" (Acts 9:15).

Lord, in spite of our sinful state, you continue to call us to go forth and make disciples of all nations; help me to be a missionary of love in all that I do and to every soul I encounter today!

Jesus: It is all for love. All emotion tends to evoke similar emotion within the person who encounters it. Be conscious of your choice to allow your emotions to flow from love and you will find that love evokes love in all situations. Simply say, "I choose love above everything, and when I stray from that intention, I choose to return to it at quickly as possible."

OCTOBER 10, 2002

"Therefore I tell you, do not worry about your life, what you will eat or drink: or about your body, what you will wear. Is not life more important than food, and the body more important than clothes? Look at the birds of the air; they do not sow or reap or store away in barns, and yet your Heavenly Father feeds them. Are you not much more valuable than they? Who of you by worrying can add a single hour to his life?" (Matthew 6:25–27).

Me: Lord, thank you for creating such beautiful flowers! Help me to focus on the essence of their beauty when I walk through the dark nights of my soul.

Jesus: What lover has ever gone so far as to create a flower with such captivating fragrance and form just to win a glance from the heart of his beloved? See the great care, love, and detail I have used to create them? I am using this same care, love, and detail to create within you a new heart and to renew a steadfast spirit within you! I love you! Lose yourself in me . . . nothing is beyond my creating hand, my renewing love, my compassionate heart. I create. I do not destroy. During the times in your life when you feel destroyed or overcome by circumstances, remember I am the creator who renews and restores even through the dark night of the soul. Some of my greatest work has taken place at night.

Just as the bulbs remain dormant in the ground through the long cold winter, so too the soul seems to exist in this dark night . . . yet life is just longing to burst forth into a new creation. Just as the bulbs multiply with each long winter, so too with the soul. With each dark night, the beauty and depth of a soul who has clung to its Savior will once again emerge with a beauty that multiplies my love all the more to the world around! Increase your confidence in me! Remain in my love, even through the longest winter . . . remain with me . . . still . . . quiet . . . waiting for the warmth of my love to stir your heart once again towards new life. Waiting for the fresh rain of my mercy to wash you clean and move you towards the surface of new life, new hope, and new love.

Consider the seed that falls into the ground. Consider its long wait before it can fulfill its purpose. My Father's timing is always perfect. Allow yourself to lose all that you are in me once again as you wait in the ground enduring this loving discipline and suffering for the sake of the new life that I am very carefully, with great love and mercy, creating within your soul. I am the lover of your soul. Can any lover give you more than I give to you? I have loved you with my very life.

Again, consider the beauty, love, and detail that bursts forth from the springtime flowers . . . all this is yours, all of this is to fill you with hope. I live in you and I died for you. My love cannot be contained in words . . . only in your heart . . . remain in me . . . the vine and the branch. Open the eyes of your soul and see all of the spiritual truths that I reveal through my creation. Know that you are surrounded by love.

October 27, 2002

"I do not understand what I do. For what I want to do I do not do, but what I hate I do. And if I do what I do not want to do, I agree that the law is good. As it is, it is no longer I myself who do it, but it is sin living in me. I know that nothing good lives in me, that is, in my sinful nature. For I have the desire to do what is good, but I cannot carry it out. For what I do is not the good I want to do; no, the evil I do not want to do—this I keep on doing. . . . What a wretched man I am! Who will rescue me from this body of death? Thanks be to God—through Jesus Christ our Lord!" (Romans 7:14–19, 24–25).

Jesus: Know your calling, my child. Be a faithful steward of all that I have given to you. Yes, I see your distress at your inability to remain in me at all times. Remember that it is the desire and the effort that I seek! Again and again, allow the Holy Spirit into the momentary wonderings of your thoughts and desires. Invite him in to help you. Remember he is the one I have given you to aid you in your weaknesses.

Me: Sweet Jesus, my weakness and propensity for sin is so great at times, it consumes me!

Jesus: No, my child, I consume you! Your momentary struggles and hardships are also consumed in me, and they are being used to achieve an eternal glory that far outweighs all the struggles and hardships that come your way.

Me: How can this be?

Jesus: My small little one, your understanding of my ways is as small as you are . . . consider the wisdom that went into creating the detail in the nature that surrounds you and that captivates your heart . . . that is only a small fragment of the depth of my riches of understanding. Trust in me more . . . go to the extent that even during your darkest hours you invite me in to make them holy. From your vantage point, my little one, you can only see smallness and limitations . . . let me take you deeper into the riches of my presence in all you do and think! You think that when you are caught in your small world of lustful thoughts or desires to control people or events that I am not present in those thoughts and desires? You enter into despair and a feeling of helplessness as if these small trials will change the depth of my love for you. No, this too is a lie from the enemy who would have you remain in your despair thinking that you are not worthy to be loved and accepted and that you are beyond my healing touch and all-consuming love. Remember, my sweet little one, you often tell your friends who are in despair, "Nothing is beyond love" . . . nothing. You read this morning about remaining in me. Lauren, even during your weakest moments when you long to possess something in the world, the fact that you are distressed about this longing . . . knowing that you will be left in a state of discontent if you obtain anything that the world has to offer . . . reveals my very presence in you! Apart from me, you can do nothing. So, anything that you pursue apart from me will always leave you with a feeling of emptiness and longing. Thank me for this!

Me: I thank you from the core of my being, sweet lover of my soul, that all roads apart from you will lead to discontent and emptiness. I am just sorry for wasting any time traveling down any of those dead ends in my life because I know what the result is. My spirit is truly willing to remain in you always, yet as you know too well, sweet savior, my flesh is so weak. Continue to stay with me always.

Jesus: There is never a moment when I am not with you. As you continue to invite me into every recess of your very being, I will continue to show you your weaknesses. I will continue to show you all longings that stem from your flesh that are apart from my heart's desire for you . . .

Me: Why is this kind of training necessary?

Jesus: Through suffering, hardships, insults, persecutions, and brokenness, love made its appeal to the world. I am love, and through suffering, I continue to draw souls into me. The same is true for all of my children. It is through the battle between the flesh and the Spirit (which will always involve sufferings) that my children are refined and purified so that they may share in eternal salvation and freedom. There is no other way, Lauren. Just think of your own small struggles; every time you choose me in them you enter into my love in a more profound way and you love more profoundly. Remember the rocks and how they were chiseled away so they would fit perfectly into the Holy Temple in Jerusalem? The chiseling only takes place when the chisel is hammered and the small piece of rock falls from the stone, ultimately leaving the stone smoother and closer to the shape it needs to be in order to fit into the Holy Temple. You are part of a Royal Priesthood, a Holy Nation, a people belonging to my Father that you may share in his eternal dwelling place . . . you are part of the body . . . my body. All parts of my body must be refined, trained, and molded so that they work together in holiness for the sake of more love in the world and freedom in the heart of mankind. Refining of any kind always involves the removal of pieces that prevent the object of refinement from reaching the goal of its master refiner and from reaching the summit of its purpose on earth. This ultimate form is the true desire of the human heart . . . yet too often, it loses its way through worldly distractions.

"But who can endure the day of his coming? Who can stand when he appears? For he will be like a refiner's fire or a launderer's soap. He will sit as a refiner and purifier of silver; he will purify the Levites and refine them like gold and silver. Then the Lord will have men who will bring offerings in righteousness" (Malachi 3:2–3).

So that you fully embrace the beautiful masterpiece that you are, you must remember that I am the refiner, the skilled artist, and you are the object of my endless talents. This can only happen through the work of my hands . . . my hands, that reflect the depth of my love for you . . . my nail scarred hands . . . a constant reminder for you that the one who is refining you unto perfection is the one whose love for you knows no limits. Let this seep into the very recesses of your soul . . . the one who is refining you loves you with a love that has no limits or conditions . . . this is why you can throw yourself at my mercy with all of your weaknesses, fears, doubts, sins . . . all that you are . . . throw into the furnace of my all-consuming mercy and love again and again. Trust that every chisel that is used to rid you of useless pieces, so that you shine like the stars in the heavens, is held in the hand that was pierced out of love for you!

Me: I feel so overwhelmed, my sweet Savior of my small soul . . . my tears flow once again out of a heart full of gratitude for taking time to commune with me . . . who am I? I didn't even have to ask you about everything my soul was yearning to hear . . . I am yours Jesus . . . I am yours! Use me, my life, my breath in spite of my continual lust for the things that the world offers . . . even take that and use it for the sake of love in this world . . . I know that is my purpose here. I give you permission to do with me according to your will . . . anything and everything needed to make my life a reflection of who you are . . . help me in my weakness . . . I am yours . . . .

Jesus: Lauren, sweet small child of ignorance, I am love to everyone! My desire to commune with you in your small state is because of who I Am . . . lose yourself in me, and you will be found once again.

Me: I just want to stay here with you Jesus . . . I feel so safe here. I won't waver in my desire for you when I am with you like this.

Jesus: With me like this? My loving creation, you are never apart from me . . . yes, when you are in the middle of your small struggles against sin, you feel distant from me because of your nature to turn against me and my ways, yet, I am always with you intimately as we are right now. Remember what you learned last year? The sky is always blue even beyond the clouds. Know that this union between our hearts is as constant—and even more constant—than the blue sky . . . more I say because it is eternal. Remember this in your struggles against sin and this will strengthen your heart: I AM and will never cease to be intimately connected to your heart!

October 29, 2002

"The Lord is faithful to all his promises and loving toward all he has made. The Lord upholds all those who fall and lifts up all who are bowed down. The eyes of all look to you, and you give them their food at the proper time. You open your hand and satisfy the desires of every living thing. The Lord is righteous in all his ways and loving toward all he has made. The Lord is near to all who call on him, to all who call on him in truth. He fulfills the desires of those who fear him; he hears their cry and saves them" (Psalm 145:13-19).

Me: Too often, I feel like a young child holding onto your hand and pulling you ahead toward different events and situations that I desire to be involved in or have an effect on, rather than walk patiently hand in hand with you as you stroll through your beautiful garden of life, pointing out all of the beauty around me. You also walk with me into situations and circumstances at a much slower pace than I like to move . . . this is training for my heart, training that is painful yet very much needed. I give you, sweet Jesus, my passion and eagerness, which all too often get in the way of your gentle loving touch that draws souls into your heart. I am simply an instrument; it is all your work. Please continue to teach me about this . . .

Jesus: Slow down, my small child . . . move with me, not in front or behind, but with me, side by side allow me to guide you gently into the circumstances and to the souls I bring your way. In this way, you are giving me permission to have my way with you and to teach you what it means to wait upon me. Silence is good, it turns the soul inward only to find me waiting to teach and gently guide its every move. Remember that I am the shepherd who gently guides his sheep. To hear and recognize my voice you must silence your own. Be still and listen.

October 30, 2002

"The Lord does not look at the things man looks at. Man looks at the outward appearance, but the Lord looks at the heart" (1 Samuel 16:7).

"Your beauty should not come from outward adornment, such as braided hair and the wearing of gold jewelry and fine clothes. Instead, it should be that of your inner self, the unfading beauty of a gentle and quiet spirit, which is of great worth in God's sight" (1 Peter 3:3–4).

Me: I take way too much time getting ready, and I worry way too much about my appearance. Help me with this.

Jesus: As often as you check your appearance in the mirror to make sure everything is in order, look into my eyes and check the appearance of your soul before me to make sure your motives and heart are in line with mine.

OCTOBER 31, 2002

"Which of you, if his son asks for bread, will give him a stone? Or if he asks for a fish, will give him a snake? If you, then, though you are evil, know how to give good gifts to your children, how much more will your Father in heaven give good gifts to those who ask him?" (Matthew 7:9–10).

Me: I have been reflecting on how much my dad loves me and constantly makes sure I know it.

Jesus: Lauren, my small one who lives in my shadow . . . you contemplate the love of your earthly father . . . I urge you to contemplate the love of your heavenly Father. Just as you have confidence that your earthly father will never withhold from you any good gift, consider how much more your Heavenly Father will bestow upon you multitudes of gifts from heaven at the very sound of your voice as you are speaking to him about your desires. Your prayers are written on my heart before you even have the chance to speak one word. Truly contemplate this . . . it comes easier for those who have been blessed with the love of an earthly father to contemplate how much greater is the love that flows from your heavenly Father . . . yet to the fatherless I say, Our love for you is greater than all the love of the fathers on earth put together. We make our home in the hearts of all souls who will have us . . . there is no child on earth who is truly fatherless or homeless within the soul. Increase your confidence in true love . . . this will aid you in your desire to be free from yourself. The greater your confidence in our love and care for you, the easier it will be for you to lose yourself in us and master your self-centeredness. There is no room for pride and selfishness in the heart that is consumed by love! Remember, you will not fail to receive many times more, fathers, mothers, sisters, brothers, and children in this age and in the age to come. Our family is limitless as is the power of the Holy Spirit who binds hearts together for eternity.

November 1, 2002

"To the weak I became weak, to win the weak. I have become all things to all men so that by all possible means I might save some" (1 Corinthians 9:22).

Me: Jesus, lover of my soul, I am so quick to turn to the flesh. You know how much I desire to be consumed by you, down to the very fiber of my existence here on earth . . . continue to change me for your glory . . . use me in every way to bring more love into the world. Increase my passion for you to the point that I truly feel an ache in my heart for all souls that have closed the door of their hearts to your sweet, gentle voice and all who feel unworthy of love and forgiveness. Teach me how to live in this world. I often feel alone and isolated because my thirst for you is so intense . . . I don't process the things in the world as the world does . . . I don't want to isolate anyone due to the awkwardness of my behavior, yet I don't want to participate either in the ways of the world. Even though I continue to fall, this is my desire: to offer myself to you for you to do with me as you wish. Help me to live in this world even though I am not of it. This can only be accomplished through your grace. How do I do this?

Jesus: With love, love in all you do. You will step into a realm of holiness that has its foundation on mercy . . . consider my life . . . I could not have been more attached to my Father's heart, yet my work of salvation was in the world. Remember my faithful servant Paul and his words you so love; he became all things to all men so that he might win some, and while he entered their world of sin, he remained holy through the desires in his heart and above all through prayer and fellowship with me in him, with me in him . . . with me in you, this is how to win souls . . . the smallest opening in the door of a broken heart is all I need for my work of salvation and love to begin restoration. May your life reflect my hunger and thirst for souls to the point that you step out of yourself and into me . . . remember . . . listen and love first then you will earn the right to speak the truth in love. Enter their world, as you desire others to enter yours. Remember it is my work and love through your small life that will win a soul over to love . . . your work is to surrender and increase your confidence in the one who calls you out of yourself into the freedom of my love . . . first for yourself and then for others.

November 2, 2002

"But you are a chosen people, a royal priesthood, a holy nation, a people belonging to God, that you may declare the praises of him who called you out of darkness into his wonderful light" (1 Peter 2:9).

Me: who am I, Lord?

Jesus: My child . . . my eager, ignorant child so full of desire and passion. Remain close to my heart in each moment I give you and I will create within you a new heart and life through our intimate union . . . you will find yourself when you lose yourself in me . . . use this knowledge to fuel your desire for intimacy with me. Think of more ways you can come to me throughout your day . . . remember I desire you more than you desire me. Who gave you your passion? You are my beautiful, passionate daughter. You flood your world with love, laughter, and hope. Be true to the woman I have called you to be. Express who you are through your laughter and love . . . live your life to the fullest in love, for love, by love. Dance your dance in the freedom of knowing you are unconditionally loved. Sing your song from the words of mercy I have written upon your soul. It is for freedom you have been set free . . . seize the moment and invite others to enter into the beautiful symphony of life and love. You are a missionary of love!

NOVEMBER 17, 2002

"For you were once darkness, but now you are light in the Lord. Live as children of light (for the fruit of the light consists in all goodness, righteousness and truth) and find out what pleases the Lord. Have nothing to do with the fruitless deeds of darkness, but rather expose them" (Ephesians 5:8–11).

Me: Jesus, I am reading about Paul and St. Augustine, and I am inspired by their sense of fortitude . . . their desire to press forward in this spiritual journey in spite of the weakness of their fleshly desires.

Jesus: All of my children are called to be set apart from this world for my purposes and are to strive for holiness! Surrender of the will is the first step in the direction of holiness. Set yourselves apart from all of the entrapments of the world. You are contemplating the lives of souls that learned the secret of the freedom of God's love . . . this practice is very good for the soul because it will increase your desire to mimic their behavior . . . their radical behavior that was set apart from the ways of the world. They were set apart or freed from desiring the things of the world . . . oh, yes, they stumbled, and they fell again and again . . . what made them holy? Again, I say to you it was their vigilant desire and search for love . . . the calmness and peace of my Father's love within their soul. They knew that his love would lead them into freedom.

You recently read about Paul's struggle against the flesh. Yes, he knew what he needed to do, yet the sin living within him constantly tripped him up in the flesh. He hungered for me, and he thirsted for my will to be done in his life in spite of his struggle with sin. This is very important for you to remember in your struggle against sin. Let the struggle inflame your hunger and thirst for the saving power of authentic love. Who will save you from your wretched state? Your savior, again and again . . . your beloved Savior if there is no sin what need do you have to be saved? Your Savior will reach down, take hold of your hand, and renew your strength for the battles you face daily. You need only to catch my eye, grab a hold of my garment, and reach out your hand or call out my name, "Jesus save me." Will I ever deny even the slightest gesture and desire for my redemptive love? To do so would be to deny myself. I am calling out for myself. I dwell in every fiber of your small existence. I am constantly calling out to myself . . . will you deny me the opportunity to love myself in you? Remember my desire for you to be in me; just as I am in the Father, all of us together united in an all-consuming bond of love with one goal: to draw the hearts of all my children into the love relationship. It is a beautiful symphony of love. If you only knew the depths of my heart . . . is there any limit to the universe? Yes! And that only exists in the hand of my Father . . . is there any limit to the depths of my most merciful heart? No, it is limitless! It is boundless! Its depths have never been reached by any man. The only restraint comes from the hardness of man's heart . . . and even that does not squelch my persistence to break through the hardness with love.

Me: Where does this hardness come from?

Jesus: Pride and ignorance, my little girl . . . pride and ignorance again and again. Yes, ignorance to the price that I have paid in order to win their hearts. If a hardened heart could witness the suffering that I endured to win it over to love, every knee would truly bow and every tongue would not cease from proclaiming me as Lord. A time will come when this ignorance will be removed and all will see me and the sacrificial gift that I offered to win their love will be clearly seen. My love will reveal the truth of my message . . . to set the captives free, to lead them out of slavery . . . slavery to the things of the world that evoke within them a continual lust for more . . . robbing them of contentment and peace.

You have experienced a small portion of my love for you my little one, this is so you can still live in this world . . . if you were consumed in the depths of the riches of my love, you would not be able to continue your day to day life skills. Your soul would be so completely awestruck that you could do nothing more than join in the continuous praises that never cease around my throne:

"Holy, holy, holy is the Lord God almighty, who was and is and is to come . . . worthy is the Lamb that was slain to receive power and wealth and wisdom and strength and honor and glory and praise!" (Revelations 4:8; 5:12).

Me: Expand my intellect, my sweet savior! I desire to know more about your heart! Let me go deeper please! Trust that I would find a way to press on in my daily task while still singing your praises without ceasing! I would like to try . . .

Jesus: You have experienced a small portion of my love . . . this is what continually draws you to my feet . . . your soul is only content when you are present to love in the moment. I give you the perfect portion of my grace that you need daily to handle all of the trials you face in your day, no more, no less. That is why I encourage you to stay present . . . for it is in the present moment that I give to you all that you need to live a life of love and freedom. I withhold from you, my little child, only what is necessary to increase your desire for more love, for more awareness of my presence within you. Do you ever go away empty handed from any of the moments we share together?

Me: No Lord . . . Never!

Jesus: Then trust me to give to you the perfect portions of all that you need for life and godliness in every moment that you walk this earth! Truly consider the examples of this kind of faith that surrounds you in nature every day . . . trust resounds through all of nature. It is known that the creator will never abandon his creation. Free yourself by embracing the reality of this truth.

Me: Thank you for your unlimited faithfulness to love. I want to remain small in you, Jesus, because then I know I am safe! People compliment me for the wisdom and knowledge of scripture that they say I have . . . I laugh because I know my place . . . this is only through your protection and grace . . . my every breath is sustained because you think of me! I am truly nothing without you in me; I own none of this. All I have comes from your heart. Anyone who shows any love for me or says a kind word of praise is truly praising you . . . you truly love yourself in all of us. People are not drawn to me but rather to your love for them through me. I give you permission to use every part of who I am for your own use . . . whatever you desire to do with me, I desire that it be done! I know that you came to give us a full life, and I entrust myself to that truth. I love you, Jesus . . . have your way with me . . . I am so humbled that you speak to me so intimately like this.

Jesus: I commune with you intimately like this because you have invited me to do so . . . or rather I should say that you surrendered to the me that lives in you . . . that continually calls out to me for unity with my love and my Father's love . . . for we are one. One in love, as you are in me and I am in the Father. The purpose is love; the call is to surrender all that you are for the purpose of love. The purpose leads to freedom. When the soul sees itself as fully loved just as it is, it is then set free to love others the same way. When the self is swallowed up, only then does the soul learn how to be loved and to love, to be known and to know. There is no room for fear of rejection.

Me: Allow me, Lord, to love myself as you love me, to forgive others and myself as you forgive me, to see myself as you see me . . . complete, beautiful, known, and loved. May this knowledge give me the desire to love others as you love me, to forgive others as you have forgiven me, and to see into others as you see into me. For this is true intimacy . . . into me see . . . a true symphony of love. Lead me on . . . oh passionate lover of my soul . . . lead me on into the freedom of your love.

December 3, 2002

"This is how God showed his love among us: He sent his one and only Son into the world that we might live through him. This is love: not that we loved God, but that he loved us and sent his Son as an atoning sacrifice for our sins. Dear friends, since God so loved us, we also ought to love one another. No one has ever seen God; but if we love each other, God lives in us and his love is made complete in us" (1 John 4:9–12).

Me: Sweet Jesus, please make me an apostle of love. May my soul be so full of you that you flow out into the souls around me. I feel overwhelmed sometimes when I think of all the souls who live against your free gift of love. Use me in all ways for their sake . . . if even for one lost soul may my heart be held prisoner for that soul . . . increase my desire for their sake . . . touch my prayer life that I may pray for their sake . . . speak your words of love and salvation through mine . . . in and of myself I am nothing! Make me an instrument of your love and mercy. Maximize my time in the mundane tasks I do so that I have more time for you and your works. Fill me up with you Jesus and may limitless love flow over into the souls you bring my way. Have your way with me.

Jesus: I listen to your cry, my little rose, I will increase your thirst for the sake of those souls who have none . . . entrust yourself to love each moment of this day.

December 10, 2002

"Commit to the Lord whatever you do, and your plans will succeed" (Proverbs 16:3).

Me: I am nothing, yet in you, I am everything... you are the bread of life and everything I need to survive. Live through me and have your way with me in all things.

Jesus: Know this: any time that you give to me will return to you ten-fold. Let go ... I will bring it to pass ... surrender ... that is your work. Let me carry you, let me carry the souls I bring your way as well ... you were never meant to carry them ... but to love them where they are. It is all my work. You are my small vessel, and I am using you to remind those around you that they are loved completely. Forget about yourself. In this way you become a vessel through which love can easily pass through.

December 12, 2002

"It is for freedom that Christ has set us free. Stand firm, then, and do not let yourselves be burdened again by a yoke of slavery" (Galatians 5:1).

Me: Make me like a child, Jesus, so that in all my friendships I will be able to love, adore, and be free from my flesh. The love I desire to give is only found in your pure heart! Love souls through me!

Jesus: The world teaches things that focus on the flesh . . . I teach things that will free you from your flesh. I make the profound simple. A child's love is free from all earthly constraints that imprison you as you grow older. A child does not consider whether or not they are loved or accepted, rather they love for the sake of love alone . . . and that is enough. Do they consider the measure they use to give to others based on whether or not they have been given to? Do they reach out and love based on the love they have received . . . no, I say their love and ability to love, in spite of what they have or have not received, is relentless and vigilant . . . the smaller they are, the more evident this truth. The Kingdom of God belongs to those who move from their hearts without fear of rejection and who are present to the great I AM and his reckless love for them. Love and confidence in love sets the human heart free from all fear!

December 14, 2002

"Consider the ravens: They do not sow or reap, they have no storeroom or barn; yet God feeds them. And how much more valuable you are than birds! Who of you by worrying can add a single hour to his life? Since you cannot do this very little thing, why do you worry about the rest?" (Luke 12:24–26).

Me: Thank you, Jesus, for those beautiful birds that flew around me today . . . they must be so free to just jump off the tree and know their wings will sustain them!

Jesus: Is there anything different for you? Are you not free in me as well? The more you jump off those things that bring you security and fulfillment in this world, the freer you will become. Jump into me . . . leave behind your perch of safety and jump into me . . . you will then experience the same freedom my little birds do . . . a freedom that only comes to those who trust in me to provide for their every need. Consider the lilies of the field and the birds in the air, they do not worry . . . they trust in my Father and live in our freedom . . . let go and you will soar within my love and mercy . . . trust me to sustain your very life. Is this not the case already? Then live freely knowing this truth.

December 19, 2002

"For I know the plans I have for you," declares the Lord, "plans to prosper you and not to harm you, plans to give you hope and a future. Then you will call upon me and come and pray to me, and I will listen to you. You will seek me and find me when you seek me with all your heart" (Jeremiah 29:11–13).

Me: What do I need to be able to let go and trust you with my future?

Jesus: Confidence . . . is that not the end for which I call you? Confidence in my ability to bring it to pass, in my ability to carry you to the exact point that I have willed for you . . . again, confidence in the ability of love to overcome all . . . even death. Increase your trust in the one who created the heavens and the earth! You often pray that my perfect plan will be accomplished in your life. Why is it that you do not then trust in me to accomplish it? Am I not the one who created the foundations of the world and the depths of the sea? Can I not also bring to fulfillment that which I have willed to be carried out in your small life? Yes . . . confidence. Strive for this my little one. Have confidence in the one who has called you by name, in the lover of your soul, in the one who was pierced out of love for you.

Again, your work here is to surrender yourself to me in all things and have the confidence in me that will give you a peace that passes all human understanding. Confidence in the world will always leave the soul disappointed and lost; confidence in me will always set the soul free.

Come closer . . . lose yourself in me only to find within yourself the fullness of the person you were created to be.

Come closer, my child, look deep within my heart, and you will find the fulfillment of your longings deep inside. Hear me speak love to you through the Holy Scriptures and allow yourself to be led by this love just as the snowflakes allow themselves to be led and gently placed by the wind.

DECEMBER 20, 2002

"Above all, love each other deeply, because love covers over a multitude of sins. Offer hospitality to one another without grumbling. Each one should use whatever gift he has received to serve others, faithfully administering God's grace in it various form" (1 Peter 4:8–10).

Me: Hold me in your lap and put within my small hands all that is needed to draw souls into your heart. I am too weak and limited in my ability to allow love to cover a multitude of sin. So I depend on you, my sweet faithful one, to give me all that I need to love deeply those souls that you send my way. I am a sinner saved by your most precious blood . . . in spite of my tendencies to fall back to the things I have done in the past, I give you permission to have me; knowing that if it weren't for your grace, I would still be lost and wondering without knowing that I have you as my shepherd to lead me into the fullness of life. I love you, sweet Jesus . . . have your way with me in all things even unto my death . . . for even death itself, in you, is swallowed up in victory . . . I have nothing to fear.

Jesus: Sweet little rose, I send you small reminders each day of my constant work for souls through your littleness. Continue to fight the fight against all fleshly attacks for the sake of souls that I have entrusted to your care . . . be faithful in all things! Never will I fail to go forth and seek out my lost sheep as I did for you. Never will I fail to completely accept those who return to the shepherd and overseer of their souls as was the case with the prodigal son. I will run to all those who show even the smallest seed of desire to walk with me throughout this life into the next. My love and desire for you is relentless and limitless. Give out to the world what flows so freely into your little heart . . . I tell you it will not cease to come back to you tenfold.

January 3, 2003

"I will give you a new heart and put a new spirit in you; I will remove from you your heart of stone and give you a heart of flesh. And I will put my Spirit in you and move you to follow my decrees and be careful to keep my laws" (Ezekiel 36:26–27).

Me: Jesus teach me. (I was ice-skating on a frozen pond.)

Jesus: My little eager one, consider how the snow falls on the cold hard ice. The ice is so cold and hard that the snow cannot penetrate it; it just sits on top of the ice. Pray hard, my child; pray for all of the hardened, cold hearts that live against me and my love and mercy . . . not knowing that the warmth of my love will melt away the cold of their pain deep within their hearts. Love and mercy continue to fall onto their cold hearts yet my free gifts are never allowed to enter in to heal and restore. Just as the sun warms the ice and the snow is absorbed, becoming part of the ice, so it is with the heart that is warmed by grace, love, and mercy . . . the hardness gives way to the transforming power of my healing touch and love bursts forth within their soul . . . so intimately that our elements become one . . . our hearts beat as one. After the snow has melted into the ice, do they then separate back into two different forms? The same holds true with divine love, it has melted into your heart and nothing can separate you from it.

JANUARY 7, 2003

"They found the stone rolled away from the tomb, but when they entered, they did not find the body of the Lord Jesus. While they were wondering about this, suddenly two men in clothes that gleamed like lightning stood beside them. In their fright the women bowed down with their faces to the ground, but the men said to them, 'Why do you look for the living among the dead? He is not here; he has risen!" (Luke 24:2–5).

Me: I often find that I look for my contentment in the superficial things of the world . . . my looks, the compliments I receive, the things I have, as well as what I accomplish.

Jesus: Once you have known my way and experienced my love and you then choose to walk in the ways of the world, know that your pain will be greater than that of the souls who have never experienced this love on earth. Remain in me, my little one, the one who is the source of true love, true peace, and true life. Why do you look for the living among the dead? Come to the one who lives and continues to love you completely. The world cannot offer life when its end is always death. Look up and arise from the flesh, focus on the things of heaven . . . love, joy, peace, patience, kindness . . . all these and more are the things that you are truly longing for . . . all of these will bring you the contentment you seek.

January 8, 2003

"All authority in heaven and on earth has been given to me. Therefore go and make disciples of all nations, baptizing them in the name of the Father and of the Son and of the Holy Spirit, and teaching them to obey everything I have commanded you. And surely I will be with you always, to the very end of the age" (Matthew 28:18–20).

Me: Lord, I feel that if I stay secluded, alone in prayer by myself then I won't offend you through sin.

Jesus: Not true, my child, by venturing out among other souls, you give the Holy Spirit the opportunity to use what you have gained through prayer and contemplation for love . . . thereby bringing clarity to your inner life.

Me: I love you Jesus! I feel that you have, for this moment in time, cleansed me from temptation for anything the world has to offer and my spirit feels free!

Jesus: Don't lose yourself in times of consolation realizing that a period of desolation may soon take you by surprise. In your peace and strength, remain conscious and aware of each moment. Stay present to my presence within you. Don't seek earthly consolation, and don't waste too much time in idle conversation, rather use your moments well . . . in training your spirit in love, mercy and humility . . . these three will protect you through any storm in life. Love the souls I bring your way, yet do not depend on them for anything other than fellowship least you find yourself disappointed that they cannot satisfy your true longings deep within your heart for eternal love. Keep your focus on the

one who quenches your thirst and satisfies your hunger. From our intimacy, you will experience free love in all other relationships . . . it is creative, limitless, and flows freely into your soul. This love always builds up and encourages because its motive is pure and simple: to love for the sake of love alone. Keep a tight rein on your flesh and its longings, remember it is never satisfied and will always want more. Rather, train your spirit to lead your flesh in all you do and you will remain peaceful in your heart. I satisfy the weary, downcast, and brokenhearted. My compassion and empathy flow from a heart that was broken out of love for you.
Me: Jesus, I love you . . . lead me on. Grant me, I pray, the grace to listen and to love . . . with reckless abandonment, as you love me.

January 24, 2003

"Commit to the Lord whatever you do and your plans will succeed" (Proverbs 16:3).

"Whatever you do, work at it with all your heart, as working for the Lord, not for men, since you know that you will receive an inheritance from the Lord as a reward" (Colossians 3:23–24).

Me: Jesus, so much of my days are filled with meaningless tasks! I get frustrated sometimes because I don't have time to do what I think is really important.

Jesus: My child, look at your worldly tasks you deem as mundane as sort of a mantra through which you lift your thoughts to me in prayer and contemplation. Just as the repetition of the prayers you often pray even the most simple, "Jesus, I love you, I want to see you," are enough to clear your head from the clutter so that you can meditate upon my life. So it is with the daily tasks of this world . . . they are a vehicle to sober the mind enough to raise the heart and mind into fellowship with love in the present moment. All moments are mine, yet many slip by without being directed to me. This is your work . . . to work as if you are working for me and in working for me, all efforts are in me and all thoughts in that work rightly belong to me . . . guide them back, my beloved child, guide all thoughts back to their rightful owner . . . remember you were bought with a price; therefore, honor me even in the most mundane humble tasks in life. Remember I was born in a stable, humble, and small; you will find me in simplicity. Honor me in all your work, in all your thoughts remembering that everything that is guided back to me results in a harvest of righteousness and a heart full of love and peace. Stay with me. Remain in me and your joy will be complete. Endless chatter between two friends connected at the heart always results in joy.

JANUARY 28, 2003

"Praise the Lord. Praise God in his sanctuary; praise him in his mighty heavens. Praise him for his acts of power; praise him for his surpassing greatness. Praise him with the sounding of the trumpet, praise him with the harp and lyre, praise him with tambourine and dancing, praise him with the strings and flute, praise him with the clash of cymbals, praise him with resounding cymbals. Let everything that has breath praise the Lord. Praise the Lord" (Psalm 150).

"Above all, love each other deeply, because love covers over a multitude of sins" (1 Peter 4:8).

Me: I was contemplating the last supper when you knew that your hour had come: Lord, you must have been filled with a great sorrow.

Jesus: Yes my little beloved one, but my love was greater! So much greater that it overcame my sorrow!

Me: Lord, I walked out of the church this morning, and a tree was filled with tons of little birds just singing away . . . they are here every morning . . . holy obedience . . . how beautiful is that? Singing your praises at sunrise! I would like to do the same for you.

Jesus: Enter in, my little one, to the symphony of endless love that surrounds you every day . . . I tell you the praises lifted to the heavens never cease!

MARCH 15, 2003
_____

"Love is patient, love is kind. It does not envy, it does not boast, it is not proud. It is not rude, it is not self-seeking, it is not easily angered, it keeps no record of wrongs. Love does not delight in evil but rejoices with the truth. It always protects, always trusts, always hopes, always perseveres . . . And now these three remain: faith, hope and love. But the greatest of these is love" (1 Corinthians 13:4–7, 13).

Me: Sometimes I base the love I give to another person on how they are loving me . . . this is such a limited way to love!

Jesus: Contemplate how you view others, how you respond to others based on how you think they view you. I stood on the hill longing to have you receive me and accept my teachings but you refused to come. I hung on the cross, I saw what you could be, what you can be . . . from this vision and understanding the alternative, I was able to say, "Father, forgive them, for they do not know what they are doing" (Luke 23:34). Do the same for your neighbor. See the good in all souls . . . create a positive attitude for them; love them deeply all the more when you get nothing in return. This is a sweet offering. An offering of love that is not based on conditions. When you lose yourself in me, my sweet child, completely lose yourself in me, it is then that you will be able to give your life for the sake of more love in the world—in spite of being loved back or received or accepted or praised. This my child is the same love that held me to the cross. This is the same cross that has led to your freedom. Freedom to love knowing that you are unconditionally loved. This love sees the best in others and has compassion on their souls when they cannot see for themselves.

Do not respond to others based on how they receive you. Respond freely from the love I put in your heart. It is then that you will be able to cover over a multitude of sins with love. My love restores, heals, and forgives. It is never moved or withheld based upon the response from the one it is offered to. Consider the conditions that I died in. I was rejected, abused, spit on . . . and love conquered all of this.

Love one another as I have loved you. Don't base your love on whether or not you are loved back. How deep can that kind of love ever go? The depths of the love in the heart that God created within man can only be seen when a man loves without any expectations. This is godly love. Again, this love held me to the cross. I did not have any expectations for you. I loved you, I forgave you, I died for you... because of who I am, not because of anything you have done. This, my little child, is true passion . . . this is true love. Offer the same kind of love to your neighbor. You will be delighted again and again at how this kind of love will flow back to your heart during your life. Allow my love to flow through your very being . . . then you will be truly free to live in me. You will be freed from the desire for approval from the desire to be received . . . from the desire to be loved by the world . . . my love will be enough! True love will set you free.

April 13, 2003

"For I am the Lord, your God, who takes hold of your right hand and says to you. Do not fear; I will help you" (Isaiah 41:13).

"So, do not fear, for I am with you; do not be dismayed, for I am your God. I will strengthen you and help you; I will uphold you with my righteous right hand" (Isaiah 41:10).

Me: (I was on a plane and the turbulence was intense) All you angels and saints! Sweet savior, allow me to live! This turbulence is out of control! Protect this flight so that I may continue to live my life and to proclaim your love and glory . . . yet, take my life if more souls will be drawn into love . . . either way, sweet Jesus, I desire to have the one that will bring the most hearts closer to yours, whether through my life or through my death . . . it is all for more love in the hearts of humanity.

Jesus: My sweet ambitious little warrior, you pray with the passion of the saints that have gone before you and who now stand before me praying that your passion for me will carry on the very mission that they lived and died for . . . the mission of love! Keep drawing from their well and you will not be able to contain yourself. Every breath you breathe out into the world will be filled with the fragrance of love, and it will draw in multitudes. The key to this aroma is to set your heart as a seal on mine so that our hearts beat together as one for the mission of love . . . love poured out into the world to free human hearts from their captive state. It is a great exodus!

Me: That's it! My heart set as a seal upon yours. Yes, my beloved savior, may your heart beat life through my veins and move me toward the goal of everlasting union with you . . . all along the journey pulling in more hearts! I love you, Jesus, and desire to have all of you. You hold the promise of everlasting life. Take away my fear of death and suffering so that nothing stands between a total gift of me to you. Thank you so much for speaking so intimately with your little soul set aflame with love for you and by you!

April 13, 2003
(later in the day)

"Therefore I tell you, do not worry about your life, what you will eat or drink; or about your body, what you will wear" (Matthew 6:25).

"Stop doubting and believe" (John 20:27).

Me: I'm worried that I will miss my connecting flight; help me to let go. This is a worldly anxiety, yet I know that anything that disturbs the peace in my heart moves your heart to respond . . . your love is so huge yet so intimately small.

Jesus: Do not doubt me! Do not doubt that I will care for your every need. If not for your own sake for the sake of all who live in constant doubt and fear, for all who live in a continual wave of anxiety . . . for their sake remain steadfast even when it seems that plans you have made will fail to reach their completion. Do not doubt that I am guiding every element that needs to be guided into the perfect position in order to accomplish my most perfect will . . . do not doubt that all things work together for good to those who love. Believe this and go forth to live it out in faith and in the freedom of love.

APRIL 16, 2003

"For we are to God the aroma of Christ among those who are saved and those who are perishing" (2 Corinthians 2:15).

Me: What kind of presence am I to be in this world?

Jesus: You are to be to the world, my little flower, a beautiful fragrance that fills the souls I bring your way with the aroma of love and mercy. You are to be a cool breeze on a hot day. Blow by each soul and refresh them with love and mercy then gently keep moving without any attachments. You belong to me so move with me in all you do and think. The winds evoke a response with everything that can be moved . . . so it is to be with you my child. Allow the gentle breezes of love to move you in and out of the lives I bring your way. Move their hearts into love and then continue on without any expectation of return. Does the wind expect to be moved by the object it moves?

Give out love and be merciful even to the souls that do not respond . . . do it because of who I am . . . because of who you are. Just as the wind blows in this or that direction because God has willed it to do so, be ready to go in any direction . . . be attentive to my voice.

April 22, 2003
_____

"A friend loves at all times" (Proverbs 17:17).

Me: Jesus, I am inspired to write about friendship today. What are friendships except for a beautiful opportunity to encourage one another's soul into love . . . a beautiful opportunity to share God's infinite graces, insights, and divine love with another soul . . . a beautiful opportunity to be Christ to another in sickness and health through times of desolation and times of consolation . . . A beautiful opportunity to be a source of love without limits, without constraint, or without weighing of thoughts to another soul. All other motives in friendship apart from love stem from ego, pride, the desire for acceptance, approval, and, in some cases, the desire to possess that which one sees as beautiful to satisfy one's fleshly appetites and fleeting desires.

All love given apart from the source of divine love is counterfeit. It is human emotion that has been twisted by Satan and used as a vehicle for self-gratification and sin.

Love from the source of love is limitless and pulls our limited human condition out into open fields of endless beauty, freedom, and joy! Just contemplate the beauty of a springtime valley filled with multitudes of wild flowers each with a different splendor yet all participating together to create a breathtaking symphony of love and beauty. Truly, a glimpse of the body of Christ . . . complimenting one another yet, at the same time, standing firm with joy and gratitude in the part that it has been called to play, without any envy or jealousy, just full of joy that it has been called to be part of such a glorious witness of love to the world!

Jesus: Yes my little wild flower . . . a valley of beautiful flowers growing side by side . . . each playing an irreplaceable part in the landscape of love!

May 6, 2003

"For everyone who asks receives; he who seeks finds; and to him who knocks, the door will be opened. Which of you, if his son asks for bread, will give him a stone? Or if he asks for a fish, will give him a snake? If you, then, though you are evil, know how to give good gifts to your children, how much more will your Father in heaven give good gifts to those who ask him!" (Matthew 7:8–11).

Me: I am not afraid to reveal to you every desire I have, knowing you are the one who calls me to do so . . . and my desires are all part of who I am.

Jesus: Notice, my child, how quickly your heart fills with the desire to pour forth love into another soul when they are hungry to receive it. Does not their desire to receive the love you have to give not increase your passion to open up the storehouses of love upon them? How much more so with me! You often ask me how can I give to you, a poor little soul, so much continuous love, mercy, and spiritual insight . . . I say to you, how can I withhold anything from an eager heart that seeks to receive all that love has to give? How can I withhold? I would have to deny my very nature to do so . . . seek and you will find; knock and the door shall be opened; ask and you shall receive. Be bold my little one, be very bold knowing that the one from whom you ask these things from is never outdone in generosity and love!

May 7, 2003

"Put your finger here; see my hands. Reach out your hand and put it into my side. Stop doubting and believe." Thomas said to him, "My Lord and my God!" Then Jesus told him, "Because you have seen me, you have believed; blessed are those who have not seen and yet have believed" (John 20:26–29).

Lauren: Lord, I desire to be closer to you. I want to see you!

Jesus: Then open your eyes and heart to the souls around you. Open up to the musical notes of love that continually play through nature. I am constantly seeking you out throughout your day. Wake-up from your slumber and you will not cease to see me in everything! My creativity in coming to you is endless!

May 8, 2003

"Not so with you. Instead, whoever wants to become great among you must be your servant, and whoever wants to be first must be slave of all. For even the Son of Man did not come to be served, but to serve, and to give his life as a ransom for many" (Mark 10:43–45).

Me: Lord, those little flowers at church today have such rich color and are so beautiful! Just as the flower exists to bring the fragrance and beauty of your love into this world, may I exist to be loved by you and to bring the fragrance of your love and mercy into the world.

Jesus: Often the smallest flowers reveal the most vibrant colors. The same is true with souls. The smaller you become, the more love will shine through you. Just as a large beam of clear light bursts into multitudes of color when passing through the smallest prism, so it is with love when it passes through a grateful, humble heart . . . it bursts into the world adding life and color to lifeless, colorless souls that encounter it. Multitudes are drawn into my heart through love, through humility and gratitude. Through brokenness comes the most profound witness of love to the world . . . let this truth strengthen your heart during your times of trouble and hardship in this world.

May 9, 2003

"Put to death, therefore, whatever belongs to your earthly nature: sexual immorality, impurity, lust, evil desires and greed, which is idolatry. Because of these, the wrath of God is coming. You used to walk in these ways, in the life you once lived. But now you must rid yourselves of all such things as these: anger, rage, malice, slander, and filthy language from your lips . . . Therefore, as God's chosen people, holy and dearly loved, clothe yourselves with compassion, kindness, humility, gentleness and patience . . . and over all these virtues put on love, which binds them all together in perfect unity" (Colossians 3:5–8, 12, 14).

Me: Lord, you say, "put to death" and "rid myself" of all the qualities within my soul that are prone to sin. Yet my question to you is how? Please know that I long to be rid of all impurity, lust, and evil desires, yet I find myself plagued by them again and again! It is by mercy and grace that I don't act upon those raging emotions within my soul and for that I will not cease to offer you praise and thanksgiving! Yet I find myself once again, after a period of peace and tranquility within, with an undivided heart in my affections for you, now in the middle of spiritual warfare . . . I feel very weak, poor, and broken, unable to fight the battle of the flesh. My desire is to take off this "old self" and put on my "new self" who you are continually renewing each day, yet I am feeling crushed by the weight of my old self. Clothe me, my sweet faithful savior, with strength and fortitude once again, least I crumble within and give into the passions of my flesh. Give me victory once again over my earthly nature. Show me your strength through my weakness.

Jesus: One thought at a time my little warrior. One thought lifted into my pierced heart. One action turned toward bringing me honor. One word spoken out of love for me. One act of holy obedience done out of a heart seeking truth. One turn of the head away from death to life. One step taken away from darkness. One more step toward the light of life. One tear shed over unfaithfulness. One cry for help in the midst of despair. One moment of grief over the weakness of man's flesh. One moment of hope knowing that death is swallowed up by life. One conviction toward choosing me over momentary pleasures of the flesh. One moment of repentance. One moment of reconciliation. One moment of freedom. All of these moments and individual choices, one at a time, will lead your heart back into mine. This is how to clothe yourself with your new life in me . . . that I am renewing in the knowledge of your Father daily. Remember this: in the midst of the toughest battles of weakness that you will face, my grace will abound all the more to sustain your heart in mine. Truly, my grace is sufficient for you and my power is made perfect through your weakness . . . make this your hope during your trials of the flesh so that you will not grow weary and lose heart! Encourage others to do the same.

May 18, 2003

"'You will seek me and find me when you seek me with all your heart. I will be found by you.' Declares the Lord" (Jeremiah 29:13).

Me: I long to have the kind of constant intimacy that my friend has with you. She seems to always be connected to your heart.

Jesus: As are you, my child . . . as are you. There is plenty of my love to go around: there is never any room for envy because the abundance of my love and grace sustain any eager soul that longs for love. Enter in and drink deeply from the waters that satisfy the thirst within. Intimacy deepens between us with each thought you raise up to my heart! Two hearts seeking each other never cease to grow closer in intimacy . . . it is no different for us except for the fact that my longing for you will always consume any small desires you have for me . . . my heart will always consume yours! Come closer.

MAY 19, 2003

"Our fathers disciplined us for a little while as they thought best; but God disciplines us for our good that we may share in his holiness. No discipline seems pleasant at the time, but painful. Later on, however, it produces a harvest of righteousness and peace for those who have been trained by it" (Hebrews 12:10–11).

Me: Lord, you continue to expand my intellect so that I can know you better. I write down as many of your insights as possible, yet I fail to be able to practice them all . . . you would think because of your constant reminders of where I need to be with you that I would be free from the flesh by now and experiencing continual inner freedom and peace.

Jesus: Oh, no, my little eager one, don't you see? Don't think of the trials and temptations you continue to walk through as a sign that deeper intimacy with love is not taking place within your soul. On the contrary, greater intimacy with love is being accomplished through the very trials and temptations that you are walking through as we speak. With each trial that I allow to remain, my purpose of refinement is being accomplished for your greater good . . . always for your greater good. So, don't lose heart in your struggle against sin. Face each temptation and trial with eager expectation and gratitude knowing that my hand is upon you, molding you through your tears and heartache into a beautiful little flower of love that will spread an even sweeter fragrance of love into the world because of the tears you shed over your decision to choose sin over me. I shed tears in the garden because of my Father's decision to choose you over sparing me the pain and anguish of my crucifixion, my tears came from the cries of the flesh not being satisfied or sparred suffering . . . the same is true for your tears; don't be afraid to let them flow . . . unite them with mine. Multitudes of hearts lose themselves to me over that kind of love. So, let your tears flow, my beloved little one, keeping your eyes fixed on the one who accomplishes his greatest work through broken and contrite hearts. Don't be afraid of the pain; let it increase your passion to press on and grab a hold of all that I am grabbing hold of you for! Use your sufferings to encourage and comfort those who suffer the same kinds of trials; stand together and encourage one another in the way of love. I refine, rebuke, and discipline those I love that they may share in holiness and walk in freedom. Holiness means to be set apart for a divine purpose; this purpose is love. Do not fear; I am with you always. The rewards will always outweigh any efforts you make to live for love! Be thankful that my love is deep enough to discipline you so that you can share in the inheritance of the saints. Don't resist it, enter in, and be changed into my likeness because of it . . . remember that I am a man of many sorrows . . . nothing is beyond me.

June 22, 2003

"Then Abraham approached him and said: 'Will you sweep away the righteous with the wicked?' . . . Then he said, 'May the Lord not be angry, but let me speak just once more. What if only ten can be found there?' He answered, 'For the sake of ten, I will not destroy it.' When the Lord had finished speaking with Abraham, he left, and Abraham returned home" (Genesis 18:23, 32–33).

Me: Jesus, how great was your love? You accepted the cross, endured the pain, and shed your blood, knowing that many would still choose fear over love . . . in spite of the free gift of love offered, many would still reject love. Yet, you still gave your whole self for the sake of any soul who would desire to turn and be healed . . . I believe that if there had been one willing soul, one soul who would turn to you, even if it was the thief on the cross, you would have still died so that they would live. You died out of a crazy, unexplainable love for us. Not because of who we were, or what we did . . . no . . . as you know, we were stooped in sin . . . you sacrificed your own life because of who you are, who your Father is in order to give birth to the gift of your love for the Father and his love for you through the Holy Spirit. You gave it all to win our hearts. Forgive us, Father, for we have sinned and we fall short of your glory, but all thanks and praise belongs to you. For while we were still sinners, you died for us, and while we are still sinning, you call us back into your heart once again. May we be worthy of such an unexplainable free gift of love and mercy. May we also have the grace to love and forgive because of who we are, not because of what any soul has done to us. I know my freedom lies in the experience of being true to my heart . . . for it is fashioned after yours.

Jesus: You are in me as I am in the Father, making your joy complete!

June 28, 2003

"Moses answered the people, "Do not be afraid. Stand firm and you will see the deliverance the Lord will bring you today. The Egyptians you see today you will never see again. The Lord will fight for you; you need only to be still" (Exodus 14:13–14).

"For everyone born of God overcomes the world. This is the victory that has overcome the world, even our faith. Who is it that overcomes the world? Only he who believes that Jesus is the Son of God" (1 John 5:4–5).

Me: I am afraid, Lord . . . of the battle . . . I pray for strength not to give in but to fight . . . fight my battle, Lord, for I am too weak . . . fight my battle for me . . . in and of myself I am void of all strength . . .

Jesus: Head into the storm, my little wild flower; head into the storm so that you will not capsize your little soul as you try to flee the pounding waves of temptations . . . keep me as your captain and allow me to guide you into still waters. Don't resist the storm; the greatest storms are used to fashion the hearts of the greatest Saints! Know that love, trust, vigilance, and perseverance are being woven into your character with each step through this storm . . . yes, I am your captain as well as the lover of your soul . . . trust in my character . . . be still and trust.

June 29, 2003

"In the same way, count yourselves dead to sin but alive to God in Christ Jesus. Therefore do not let sin reign in your mortal body so that you obey its evil desires. Do not offer the parts of your body to sin, as instruments of wickedness, but rather offer yourselves to God, as those who have been brought from death to life; and offer the parts of your body to him as instruments of righteousness. For sin shall not be your master, because you are not under law, but under grace" (Romans 6:11–14).

Me: Jesus, I confess to you every thought, word, and deed that is done and said for selfish gain and for self-gratification . . . forgive me.

Jesus: Just as you are instructed to drink plenty of water after a deep massage in order to rid your body of all the impurities . . . so it is with the soul after confession. Drink me in, seek me out . . . be even more diligent in taking in the Scriptures and filling your soul with many prayers so that you will continue the cleansing process of all impurities that reside in the flesh and infect the soul. Flush them out of your system and allow the fragrance of my love and forgiveness to penetrate deeply through bone and marrow into the depth of your soul, making all things beautiful. Go and sin no more, fill up what is still lacking so that you do not grow weary in your struggle against sin. Store the Holy Scriptures within your heart and ask the Holy Spirit to help them take root, changing you from the inside out . . . fashioning you into me . . . I desire to have my way with you in all things. Always be willing to be moved by me for I am always willing to move you.

Heed Me . . . knowing I have the best in store for you . . . I will never be outdone in generosity! Be willing to part with everything knowing that whatever you leave behind in order to gain more of me will not fail to return to you tenfold . . . heed me . . . lay everything down . . . my storehouses are always full of life and love! Lean into me . . . lean into me.

July 2, 2003

"Because of the Lord's great love we are not consumed, for his compassions never fail. They are new every morning; great is your faithfulness" (Lamentations 3:22).

Me: Lord, do you ever tire of forgiving me of the same offenses again and again?

Jesus: No, my little one, never do I tire of giving you the opportunity to come unto me yet another time . . . my forgiveness is constantly extended to you . . . it is very accessible in order to encourage your heart to come back to mine and to know yourself. Each time you come back to me you are fashioned once more into my likeness . . . holiness being the goal, being set apart for love. Make this your daily vocation: to choose love over fear yet another time. Your resolve to go and sin no more will become all the more intense as will the quickness of your desire to run into my forgiving arms once again. Remain with me longer the next time you are tempted to stray. If children lost sight of their goal to walk, you would all be crawling. Do not focus on the fall . . . focus on the pursuit of the walk . . . the journey of life and love. Is it not true that every fall reveals more truth about who you are and the person you desire to be? Embrace it all . . . it is all being used to draw you closer to the person you were created to be!

July 5, 2003

"Dear friends, let us love one another, for love comes from God. Everyone who loves has been born of God and knows God. Whoever does not love does not know God, because God is love. This is how God showed his love among us: He sent his one and only Son into the world that we might live through him. This is love: not that we loved God, but that he loved us and sent his Son as an atoning sacrifice for our sins. Dear friends, since God so loved us, we also ought to love one another. No one has ever seen God; but if we love each other, God lives in us and his love is made complete in us" (1 John 4:7–12).

Me: Have all my love, Jesus . . . all my love . . . yet it is so limited, so I beg you to fill up my heart to the brim with limitless love so that the love I can give to other souls will be complete. Thank you, Jesus . . . no words can express my gratitude to you . . . for you . . . you have given to me your heart . . . your love and most importantly intimacy with you . . . I am so filled at this moment in time with the awareness that you love me . . . You love me . . . through and through . . . if this is the only moment in time of this awareness you have blessed me with then I will renew my hope daily in this truth . . . only by your grace . . . but for now, I give to you every tear that so easily flows from my small soul for the sake of all souls who refuse this perfect love because of doubts and fears . . . I desire to stay here forever . . . you and me . . . allow me to carry a portion of the weight of desire that you hold in your heart to draw human hearts into the experience of love.

Jesus: All for love, my little warrior, all for love!

July 9, 2003

"A servant girl saw him seated there in the firelight. She looked closely at him and said, 'This man was with him.' But he denied it. 'Woman, I don't know him,' he said. A little later someone else saw him and said, 'You also are one of them.' 'Man, I am not!' Peter replied. About an hour later another asserted, 'Certainly this fellow was with him, for he is a Galilean.' Peter replied, 'Man, I don't know what you're talking about!' Just as he was speaking, the rooster crowed. The Lord turned and looked straight at Peter. Then Peter remembered the word the Lord had spoken to him: 'Before the rooster crows today, you will disown me three times.' And he went outside and wept bitterly. (Luke 22:56–62).

Me: My beloved one, I was reflecting on how close I felt with you on my birthday. The graces you poured into my heart were enough to completely captivate my soul . . . I did not want the moment to end . . . you allowed me to experience the depth of your love for me, and I was completely in awe of you . . . how then can I so quickly revert to the thoughts of the flesh the next day after experiencing such connection with you? Forgive me for my inability to remain enthralled by you and for turning back to the ways of the world after you share such deep spiritual insights with me.

Jesus: My precious little wild flower . . . yes, you are wild at heart, my love. Allow me to calm the storms that blow so quickly through your soul with the balm of my love and the calming touch of my hand. Consider your brother Peter . . . yes, the "Rock" to whom I entrusted the keys of my kingdom to . . . Peter . . . passionate wild at heart Peter . . . so eager to have me wash his whole body. So eager to protect me from the very act that would save his own soul. So eager to protect and fight for the safety of his beloved savior. So eager to walk on top of water yet so quick to sink because of his lack of faith. So eager to jump in the water and swim to his Savior. Yes, My sweet, passionate Peter, so eager to have all of me and so eager to give all of himself to me in spite of himself, not even aware that he would one day have the opportunity to do so.

My sweet child, Peter ate with me at table, shared in the Paschal Supper, where I was the sacrificial lamb offered up for the sake of salvation of souls. Peter shared my bread, my wine, my ministry, my passion. He saw what you did not; he witnessed what you only imagine as you read the Sacred Scripture. Peter was there . . . yes, you would think because of all he witnessed and experienced first-hand with his beloved Lord that he would be incapable of denying the one he professed to love . . . three times . . . yet his concupiscence and his depth of despair over the weakness of his flesh along with his hunger to reconcile to my heart enabled his little passionate soul to soar to the heights of my love poured out into the world beyond his wildest dreams. He had a depth of passion for reconciliation to my heart that led him to a conviction that would one day be enough to hold him to the cross out of love for me. I ask you . . . are you greater than my servant Peter that after experiencing intimacy with me that you are incapable of wondering back into the sin of the flesh? Increase your confidence in what I will do through your weak state . . . increase your confidence through the humiliation of your weaknesses and your inability to stay with me. Let your moments of weakness move you to rely more fully on the one who calls you to faithfulness . . . I will do the work I call you to in spite of yourself. Humility, my child . . . remember you are nothing without me as was Peter, yet with me, there are no limitations to your work . . . give yourself over completely to love . . . hold nothing back, even your sinful inclinations . . . offer them to me as well so they do not overtake you. Is there anything offered to me that cannot be overcome and made beautiful? Don't ever think your sin is beyond my grace, for that was the very thought that caused Judas to take his life. My blood, poured out to win your heart, covers a multitude of sin.

Increase your confidence in me and humble yourself enough to know that no temptation has seized you except for what is common to man . . . I am faithful . . . come back to me once again . . . reconcile your heart to mine and go forth with an even greater passion to witness love and mercy to souls lost in the despair of sin thinking their sin is beyond my love. Out of the depths, I will call you by name! Come forth and be reconciled once again to my heart. Listen to my voice . . . Lauren, do you love me? Then feed my sheep . . . Lauren, do you love me? Then tend my flock . . . Lauren, do you love me? Then feed my lambs. Reconcile to my heart once again my little passionate wild flower. Is there anyone here to condemn you? Then go and sin no more.

July 14, 2003

"Not that I have already obtained all this, or have already been made perfect, but I press on to take hold of that for which Christ Jesus took hold of me. Brothers, I do not consider myself yet to have taken hold of it. But one thing I do: Forgetting what is behind and straining toward what is ahead" (Philippians 3:12–13).

Me: Lord, I don't feel worthy of the call to a vocation of love. I am weak . . . I don't deserve anything . . . help me, Jesus. The world is drowning out my ability to see myself as you see me.

Jesus: My weary little warrior, do not give in, do not give up . . . stay the course even if you should feel that you will drowned in your fleshly desires, I say to you keep pressing on in spite of the intense trial. Your flesh will always cry out in pain when you are denying it something it craves in order to remain with me . . . yet the reward that awaits you for every act of obedience far exceeds any momentary pain or sadness you may endure during the storm. Do not fear the pain that accompanies the struggle . . . remember it was pain that was endured that resulted in salvation . . . this is always the case. Allow me to guide you safely into green pastures . . . you are in the midst of tribulation…allow it to strengthen your fortitude and increase your vigilance in your decision to choose me over the ways of the world.

Remember that sanctity comes from the most tumultuous storms of the soul. When all is well with the soul, where is the opportunity for growth and advancement? Hardships, trials, and temptations should be looked upon as opportunities to learn the art of allowing, presence, humility, gratitude, and freedom. Increase your confidence in the one who is calling you! Let go!

July 16, 2003

"Humble yourselves, therefore, under God's mighty hand, that he may lift you up in due time. Cast all your anxiety on him because he cares for you. Be self-controlled and alert. Your enemy the devil prowls around like a roaring lion looking for someone to devour. Resist him, standing firm in the faith, because you know that your brothers throughout the world are undergoing the same kind of sufferings. And the God of all grace, who called you to his eternal glory in Christ, after you have suffered a little while, will himself restore you and make you strong, firm and steadfast. To him be the power for ever and ever. Amen" (1 Peter 5:6–11).

Me: Lord, I am overwhelmed by your generosity toward me in the midst of my struggle . . . I long to be seen and pursued by my husband . . . Definition: Intimacy—see into me. I am longing to connect; I feel so disconnected to the man I should feel most connected to . . .

Jesus: Is not my love limitless and unconditional? My generosity is not dependent on the holiness of your soul but on the very center of who I am. In fact, at some of your weakest moments of struggle, temptation, and hardship, I will often pour out an overabundance of generosity that will take various forms in your life in the hope of winning you over once again to my heart . . . in the hope of moving your heart out of the depth of despair and into the light of my forgiveness and grace! Know that love is accomplishing a greater purpose within your soul that will far outweigh any efforts and tears that your battle evokes within you. I withhold only to push a soul to the point of surrender in areas that have become idols and addictions; remember . . . I am a jealous God, I will not settle for only portions of your heart and will go to great extremes to win all of you. Once the soul surrenders to love and trust, often due to exhaustion and discouragement, the floodgates of generosity fill the soul with such force that all of the grief and sadness experienced during the battle become swallowed up in love and mercy. The results include: endurance, fortitude, compassion, humility, love, acceptance, and internal freedom. Do not resist the struggle . . . enter in with confidence knowing that all things will work together for you because you are called according to my purposes . . . I will never tire of reminding you of your identity in this world. What I will always comes to pass . . . don't resist my will . . . draw closer to my heart and enter in . . . especially now when you are in such need and distress . . . let me shepherd your heart back home. Allow me to lead you beyond your wants and needs into the freedom of acceptance and love. Pray constantly.

Invite me into each moment and watch the beauty that results from the touch of the hand that carries the wounds of pure love for you.

July 17, 2003
_____

"You do not support the root, but the root supports you. You will say then, 'Branches were broken off so that I could be grafted in.' Granted. But they were broken off because of unbelief, and you stand by faith. Do not be arrogant, but be afraid. For if God did not spare the natural branches, he will not spare you either. Consider therefore the kindness and sternness of God: sternness to those who fell, but kindness to you, provided that you continue in his kindness. Otherwise, you also will be cut off. And if they do not persist in unbelief, they will be grafted in, for God is able to graft them in again" (Romans 11:18–23).

Me: I have no words to express my hunger and thirst for you to love through me with your love so that my love is pure and builds up the hearts of my brothers and sisters. May I never be a stumbling block to them. Please help me, Jesus.

Jesus: Remember, my passionate little soul, it is all my work, all my work! Even when you stumble, do you think that I am not able to restore in an instant what you have weakened through your fallen nature? Remember the thief on the cross?

Me: Lord, please take my life before I would offend you so much so that I should be cast away from your heart like a dead branch that has lost all life and sensitivity to life because it has been swallowed up by the world and can no longer be used for anything but to be thrown into the fire. I am worried that because of my deep feelings of rejection that I am experiencing in my marriage that I will act out my pain in a destructive way.

Jesus: Increase your confidence! My little doubting Thomas, increase your confidence! Do you not know me? I shed my blood to increase your confidence in my love for you. It is my love and mercy alone that moves a soul to go and sin no more. Begin again . . . over and over and over . . . begin again with me . . . leave the moments in the past and press on to take a hold of the life I am calling you to embrace. Satan would have you die in the grief of your sin as did Judas . . . rise up and walk! I am calling you out of the darkness into light . . . hear me calling your name and move forward.

SEPTEMBER 2, 2003

"I run in the path of your commands, for you have set my heart free. I will walk about in freedom, for I have sought out your precepts" (Psalm 119:32, 45).

Me: Lord, I want to be free. I feel like I have been pursuing intimacy all of my marriage and I have never gotten there. I feel like I can see it through a glass window and I am a bird that continually flies toward it, yet again and again I hit the glass only to fall paralyzed once again to the ground with broken wings. I feel like I am trying to squeeze lemon juice from a banana!

Jesus: Oh, Lauren, once you let go of all of your desires and vain pursuits to gain those things you feel will satisfy the longings of your heart and focus all of your energy on loving and accepting yourself, staying present in each moment, loving those around you, constant prayer and doing all you do with your heart set on love, you will find freedom. You will soar to new heights because your eyes are not on your own condition but on the things of heaven.

If the bird was captivated by her own wings and could not take her eyes off them, she would never learn to fly. It is only when she looks out to the horizon that her body is moved from within to do that which she was created to do. Look within and then look out of yourself . . . look to the souls around you. Reach in and then reach out. Fix your eyes on the author and perfecter of your faith. I will lead you on beyond yourself into the freedom and wisdom that comes from acceptance and love . . . with this vision, your soul will soar. Leave what is behind and press on toward the goal to win the prize. Open your eyes and look around you.

See all of the potential for learning and growth that continually surrounds you daily. Grab a hold of each moment and plunge yourself into the present. The more you let go, the higher you will go in your spiritual awareness and the freer your soul will become to be all that you are called to be . . . your higher self that is continuously beckoning you toward new horizons, new experiences, and your fullest potential that you were born to discover. Spiritual awareness is most acute in the present moment and in surrender. Contemplate the bird before it leaps into the air . . . completely present, fully surrendered, and recklessly confident in its born potential. The bird's only contemplation is that of remaining present to its born potential and then acting on it. You must do the same. Occupy your entire being. Raise your awareness of your being rather than being caught up in the doing of life . . . remember Mary and Martha? Mary was a human being . . . Martha was a human doing. Remember who you are . . . a human being. Remain present moment to moment . . . and the doing of life will unfold beautifully!

September 14, 2003

"If you belonged to the world, it would love you as its own. As it is, you do not belong to the world, but I have chosen you out of the world" (John 15:19).

Me: I feel burdened by what I accomplish or don't accomplish in my day. I have given it permission to dictate my sense of self-worth. If I get all of my tasks done then I am worthy of self-love and acceptance . . . if I don't then I have fallen short and I don't deserve love and acceptance . . . Is that crazy or what? I have attached my sense of well-being to what I do and don't do . . . *and* how well I do it! I also feel that I need to earn the right to relax, sit back, and simply be . . . what is that all about? I have given the worldly things and accomplishments the power to make me feel good about myself.

Jesus: Don't be so quick to check on your attachments to the world, rather be quicker to check your attachment to my heart . . . with worldly attachments come jealousy, fear, anxiety, and worry because once you have obtained that which you seek to be attached to you are then plagued by the fear of losing it. You will never lose the love that flows from my heart into yours . . . that is eternal, complete, and free. Let go of your desire to own and control people and things in this life. Enjoy them but do not attach your sense of self-worth and well-being to them . . . if you do, you will experience much disappointment and anxiety in this life. Your self-esteem comes from your awareness that you are completely loved just as you are . . . that you are complete without any worldly accomplishment. Then you can love others and multiply the gifts you have been given within out of the fullness of heart rather than the neediness of feeling that you are incomplete. Your sense of self-worth always flows from inside of you. You never find it outside of your being . . . and if you feel that you do, it is only temporary. As soon as the excitement and glamour wears off you are left with a feeling of emptiness and desperation for more temporary gratification. It is a vicious cycle. Any attention you give to your inner state of being for the purpose of enlightenment in the ways of unconditional love . . . for God, yourself, and others . . . will be returned to you tenfold. Contentment and love walk hand in hand.

SEPTEMBER 17, 2003

"For the Lamb at the center of the throne will be their shepherd; he will lead them to springs of living water. And God will wipe away every tear from their eyes" (Revelation 7:17).

Me: When fly-fishing, I was contemplating how clear the stream remained even after flowing over dirt and rocks.

Jesus: Just as the clear waters flow over the rocks, cleansing and refining yet remaining clear, how much more it is with my blood that flows over a multitude of impurities, cleansing, and refining yet remaining untouched by the dirt of sin. All sin that it washes over becomes cleansed, never leaving a trace of its existence behind. A soul purified by my blood emerges as clean as the streams of water that flow from the highest peaks . . . even more so. Herein lays your confidence to enter into me with all of your impurities, failings, and dirt, knowing you shall go forth cleansed and renewed. Make this your reason for going and sinning no more. My blood cleanses completely, my mercies never fail, and love begs you to stay close to my heart. Come all who are weary and burdened by the weight of sin; allow the freedom of divine love to give you rest in forgiveness and a profound sense of self-worth and freedom.

SEPTEMBER 20, 2003

"Who shall separate us from the love of Christ? Shall trouble or hardship or persecution or famine or nakedness or danger or sword? . . . For I am convinced that neither death nor life, neither angels nor demons, neither the present nor the future, nor any powers, neither height nor depth, nor anything else in all creation, will be able to separate us from the love of God that is in Christ Jesus our Lord" (Romans 8:35, 38–39).

Me: Lord, is there a sin I could commit that would make me beyond your love?

Jesus: Nothing can separate you from my love . . . nothing. Knowing this should increase your resolve to remain in me. Does a lover take advantage of his beloved knowing that they can be assured of their forgiveness? What kind of love would that be? One that is based on selfish gain not on true love. True love protects, honors, and cherishes its beloved one, making every effort not to offend the one it has entrusted its heart to . . . so it must be with me . . . if in fact you are entrusting your heart to me, knowing I have entrusted you with the last beat of my heart. Be careful then to guard yourself against anything that may come between us. Remember the knife of sin . . . make every effort to protect your heart from being severed from mine. Remain, remain, and remain. Should you stumble because of the concupiscence of your poor flesh then get up quickly and run to me so as not to miss out on a moment of our intimacy. Allow my love to wash you clean and increase your resolve to stay with me longer next time around . . . I know your weak state . . . never lose heart . . . I hunger and thirst for you to come back to my heart even before you realize that you are gone. Come to me, stay with me . . . even if it is one moment longer today than yesterday . . . come! Nothing is beyond love.

SEPTEMBER 25, 2003

"'Because he loves me,' says the Lord, 'I will rescue him; I will be with him in trouble, I will deliver him and honor him. With long life will I satisfy him and show him my salvation" (Psalm 91:14–16).

Me: Lord, you amaze me that you continue to sustain me in you in spite of my selfishness and sinful tendencies. I feel like I want to run from the pain in my heart.

Jesus: Why should it take you by surprise that my mercies and love continue to flow in spite of the fallen condition of your soul when while you were still sinning? I died for you, and while you continue to stumble along this path of life, I continue to awaken love within you daily, knowing that you would be crushed under the weight of your own guilt . . . I set you free daily. In spite of your concupiscence, my love will continue to flood your soul, not because of anything you do but because of what I have already done for you. The fact that you continue to come back to me, and quicker every time, is proof that my work is being accomplished within your soul. Rejoice then in your temptations and sufferings knowing with full confidence that they are being used as tools to fashion your heart after mine . . . for it was through great suffering and trial that salvation was born into the souls of men . . . the same holds true today. I delight in the offering of desire for more of me!

SEPTEMBER 26, 2003
─────────────

"He makes clouds rise from the ends of the earth; he sends lightning with the rain and brings out the wind from his storehouses" (Psalm 135: 7).

Me: Oh, Lord, I know you opened all of those roses so beautifully, so perfect as a sign to me of your undying love. The roses continue to get more beautiful with each passing day!

Jesus: Just wait and see what I do with your heart, as I gently open it up to my love with each passing day. The beauty of the rose will fade away, yet the work I do on the human heart is eternal and the brilliance of its splendor grows more captivating with each passing day. Allow me to unfold your heart into mine!

OCTOBER 26, 2003

"You, however, are controlled not by the sinful nature but by the Spirit, if the Spirit of God lives in you. And if anyone does not have the Spirit of Christ, he does not belong to Christ. But if Christ is in you, your body is dead because of sin, yet your spirit is alive because of righteousness. And if the Spirit of him who raised Jesus from the dead is living in you, he who raised Christ from the dead will also give life to your mortal bodies through his spirit, who lives in you" (Romans 8:9–11).

"Totally love him who gave himself over totally for love of you." —St. Clare

Me: Jesus, my beloved, free me from my desire to satisfy my sense of well-being with things of the flesh . . . forgive me for searching to satisfy my deep longings to be cherished and adored in my flesh rather than seeking consolation from your heart. The flesh is never satisfied as it is a restless poison that continuously searches the earth to possess that which can only be obtained in spirit . . . so it is relentless in its pursuit of contentment searching aimlessly to grab hold of the things which turn and devour . . . leaving the body wounded, broken, confused, and aching for more of that which will destroy and leave only emptiness and grief. But the Spirit brings life to all it touches. When the will chooses to pursue the things of the Spirit a flood of contentment and satisfaction permeates the deepest recesses of the soul . . . lifting one out of the endless pit of dissatisfaction that accompanies the pursuit of the flesh. Yes, we are spiritual beings having a physical experience. Therefore, it makes sense to allow the spirit to guide the flesh into all things.

The spirit places the soul on solid ground that does not shift like the sinking sands of the fleshly world.

Why wander then to those things that cause pain? I am confident that our choice to sin causes pain in your heart, Jesus, not so much because of the actual act of disobedience, your mercy is always willing to forgive and cleanse a repentant heart, but rather because of the pain, sadness and grief you know will accompany the sin. You weep over our choice to sin because you see the tears we will shed and the ache in our heart when we are left empty-handed and wounded after our choice to satisfy our longings for love with those things that ultimately will corrode our hearts and lives.

Jesus: Look deeply into the wisdom of your heart. Listen to your heart, Lauren, for out of it flows the springs of life and the freedom you seek.

NOVEMBER 13, 2003

"But God chose the foolish things of the world to shame the wise; God chose the weak things of the world to shame the strong. He chose the lowly things of this world and the despised things—and the things that are not—to nullify the things that are, so that no one may boast before him" (1 Corinthians 1:27–28).

Me: Lord why do you continue to use me to witness your love to the world when I am caught up in the things that tie me down to the world? It seems that the more you allow me to experience the weakness of my flesh and the poor choices I continue to make, the greater my witness seems to be. Why?

Jesus: My little flower. I know what you desire to be for me . . . this is what I move through, not your poor choices but your desire for love in all things . . . your desire for holiness. Am I not your savior? Then allow me to save you from your sinful inclinations . . . is this not what I died for? I have chosen in the past those souls who have been stooped in sin to accomplish my greatest works. Remember, I choose the weak things to shame the wise. Why? Because these souls are easily moved by love. They long to be set free from their confusion and discontent; therefore, they gravitate toward mercy and grace with a fervent expectation of deliverance. Are you not more hungry and thirsty deep within when you are deprived from your food source? The same is true with those who have stumbled in their faith walk . . . their hunger for holiness and truth grows with a greater intensity than if they had not fallen. I use all things for my glory. Increase your confidence. See yourself as I do . . . as you are, not as you should be . . . I make all things new!

I reward you for your desires and efforts not your successes. I am all love . . . all mercy . . . I continue to reach out to you with a love that knows no condition . . . it has nothing to do with your own efforts that I adore you. I adore you because I am in you and you are in me . . . love begets love . . . ask for more!

NOVEMBER 24, 2003

"'You still lack one thing. Sell everything you have and give to the poor, and you will have treasure in heaven. Then come, follow me.' When he heard this, he became very sad, because he was a man of great wealth" (Luke 18:22–23).

Me: I am attached to so many things in the world! If I sold everything I had, sadly, I think I would lose my sense of identity.

Jesus: Treasure in heaven comes when you live your life unattached to things you possess. The only thing I want you to be attached to is my heart. The love given and received from my heart is eternal . . . all other things will pass away. Along with any other attachment comes fear, jealousy, and anxiety over the thought of losing that which you have attached yourself to . . . so I say . . . live without attachment, love without attachment and your soul will move through this life free from the burdens that tie you down to those things that will ultimately steal your joy. Contemplate the joy that you feel deep within when the beauty of a rose or sunset captivates your heart . . . are you attached to that experience? No, you are simply caught up in the appreciation of beauty and creativity without the need to control or own it . . . love this way and you will be set free from the many anxieties that weigh you down in life.

January 10, 2004

"May God himself, the God of peace, sanctify you through and through. May your whole spirit, soul and body be kept blameless at the coming of our Lord Jesus Christ. The one who calls you is faithful and he will do it"
(1 Thessalonians 5:23–24).

Jesus: Let nothing disturb you except an increased hunger to love better.

Me: Lord, how can I love others better?

Jesus: By forgetting yourself . . . this way—more of me, less of you . . . this will lead you into the purity of love that you desire to offer the souls that I have entrusted to your care. Trust that you are taken care of completely . . . let go and trust that you are safe and whole!

Me: Jesus, I am sorry for not being a better steward of all you have entrusted me with. I feel like I've used the things of the world even people to help me feel more secure about who I am, and yet I continually feel a sense of discontent whenever I turn to the world over you.

Jesus: My little one, give thanks that you are even aware of your weak condition for this knowledge comes not from the earth but from your Father in heaven, who loves you enough to make you aware of your need for my ways in your life. Increase your gratitude for each breath in life and for every truth that is written on your heart . . . for it is in truth that you clearly see yourself as you are . . . this is true humility . . . to see oneself as you truly are . . . the love from the heavenly realm is so great that you are seen as you desire to be . . . always desire for more of me in you. You have not because you ask not . . . ask . . . ask for the things of heaven and you shall receive in abundance! Lose yourself in me more today than yesterday . . . my love is enough for both of us! Your sense of security in who you are will never come from people or things. Your authentic sense of self flows from all things unseen . . . you must focus on your internal awareness of who you are . . . not the external awareness of who you are . . . move from the inside out!

January 11, 2004

"Commit to the Lord whatever you do, and your plans will succeed" (Proverbs 16:3).

Me: Today, I started out thinking of your love for me. I invited you into everything I did and everything unfolded perfectly, just like a beautiful rose.

Jesus: Why should it surprise you that your day has been so productive and your heart so full of love and joy when you have invited me into every moment today? I will never be outdone in generosity . . . just as a thoughtful guest brings a gift to the host of the celebration; I come with gifts beyond compare when you invite me into the home of your heart. I am the tender, gentle compassionate guest who never stops giving. Make my ways, your ways.

January 12, 2004

"Whatever you do, work at it with all your heart, as working for the Lord, not for men" (Colossians 3:23).

Me: I have nothing, Lord . . . nothing to give you today.

Jesus: You have me and that is everything! Borrow from my heart and you will never be lacking.

Me: Lord, how can doing dishes bring you honor?

Jesus: It's not the task as much as it is the heart in the work. A task done in haste comes to nothing. If love flows into the work and through the heart in prayer, it becomes an offering that lasts forever. Do everything with me and for me just like the flowers in your garden . . . they lack nothing . . . everything they do blooms from the intention of bringing more beauty into the world.

April 15, 2004

"He went down with them and stood on a level place. A large crowd of his disciples was there and a great number of people from all over Judea, from Jerusalem, and from the seacoast of Tyre and Sidon, who had come to hear him and to be healed of their diseases. Those troubled by evil spirits were cured, and the people all tried to touch him, because power was coming from him and healing them all" (Luke 6:17–18).

Author Note: This entry is particularly profound for me because it was written two years before I was diagnosed with cancer. I have emerged from this experience more real, authentic, and emotionally free than any other time in my life.

Me: Lord, it has been too long since recording my thoughts. I love you so much. My soul is being stripped of everything these days. I just had a dream last night. You were the divine physician . . . I was very sick and dying . . . my family rushed me to the hospital, and you began to operate on me. It was very painful at first . . . I felt myself slipping from this world and you brought me back with the care of your gentle hands. You worked very quickly and healed within me everything that was causing me to lose my life. You are the divine physician, and I feel strongly that I am about to enter into the skillful work of your hands upon my injured soul confident that your touch and expertise will leave me in a lot better condition than before my sickness. Help me always to remember that you are the gentle healer. I know I have much to learn about being real in this life, about expressing who I am without fear of rejection, about living from the foundation of love rather than fear . . . I feel that the sufferings of life though painful for a while ultimately produce a stronger more *real* and vibrant character within the soul. Give me the strength never to fear suffering knowing that the results will always outweigh the pain. Help me not to forget this during my life on earth. Heal me, Lord, for I know not the full extent of the sickness I need to be healed from but I trust that you do.

July 25, 2004

"Love your neighbor as yourself" (Matthew 19:19).

Me: Lord, bring me back into you. I feel so self-absorbed.

Jesus: You are coming back, my little one, one step at a time. In order to die to yourself and take up your cross to follow me, you must enter into yourself for a time. You must know yourself in order for true surrender of self to take place. Embrace these moments of self-discovery, as they will strengthen and enable you to give more to the world around you. Do not be anxious at the thought that you are self-absorbed; rather embrace this time with an eager expectation knowing that an even deeper level of intimacy with life awaits you as a result of your work to "know thyself." I must add that you must then strive to love, with my help, all that you discover about the depths of who you are . . . your strengths as well as your weaknesses, your achievements as well as your failings. My child, just think of the freedom that awaits you when you come to fully love and accept all that you are . . . it is only then that you can enter into the true meaning and experience of loving your neighbor and your God as you love yourself . . . freely and completely. This is how I love you. See yourself as I see you . . . worthy of all that I have to give because you are created in the image of my beloved Father, wonderfully and beautifully created . . . by love, in love, and for love.

July 26, 2004

"'Come, follow me,' Jesus said" (Matthew 4:19).

Me: I will change my ways, not because I know it's right but because I want to embrace the lifestyle that embraces love as its cornerstone . . . no longer will my life control me, people, and circumstances; I will control my life and God controls me . . . in this lies my freedom from bondage. I choose life and I choose love.

Jesus: You have the choice to live out the truth of this statement every day.

SEPTEMBER 27, 2004

"Moses said to God, 'Suppose I go to the Israelites and say to them, 'The God of your fathers has sent me to you,' and they ask me, 'What is his name?' Then what shall I tell them?' God said to Moses, 'I am who I am. This is what you are to say to the Israelites: 'I AM has sent me to you.'" (Exodus 3:13–14).

Me: You choose to stay in the present moment. That is so hard for me to do sometimes, yet I know I will find you most profoundly in the *now*.

Jesus: I AM. Meditate on being present. Did I not say, I AM? not I wAS or I wILL BE but I AM. You will find me in the present moment. Be still and know that I AM. I know you are going through a crucible of your heart. Do not fail to remember that I am faithful . . . invite me into each moment . . . let go of the past . . . trust me with your future . . . do you not know that my plans for you will ultimately fulfill the deepest desires of your heart? You often ask for things that will cause you more pain than joy. I love you enough to overlook your ignorance. I deprive you of current requests in order to give to you what you truly crave . . . what you truly need for true life. The kind of gift that will lead you to sing once again with conviction deeper than before. Rejoice in the Lord! His love endures forever; his faithfulness extends to all generations! Surrender my child . . . surrender, abandon, trust, and receive . . . freedom, hope, and above all love.

FEBRUARY 22, 2005

"Do not store up for yourselves treasures on earth, where moth and rust destroy, and where thieves break in and steal. But store up for yourselves treasures in heaven, where moth and rust do not destroy, and where thieves do not break in and steal. For where your treasure is, there your heart will be also" (Matthew 6:19–21).

Me: Jesus, I want to be loved and desired by my husband. The pain is too deep to face. Help me find my way to peace. I am wondering if I should become a married nun to make sense of the lack of intimacy in my marriage . . . Is that even possible?

Jesus: When love is lifted up to heaven, it becomes eternal. When it is held onto for selfish reasons or for self-gratification, it will eventually die . . . lifted up it is multiplied and defies time and space. For all that is stored up in the heart full of love becomes a treasure in heaven where moth and rust will never destroy and thieves can never break in and steal. So continue, my child, as difficult as it is to store up for yourself treasures in heaven. Although the ultimate gratification is delayed, the reward far outweighs the momentary pain that infiltrates into the waiting time. Increase your confidence! Have I ever failed you? I am the heart where all love is formed, given, and received. Can the creator of love, the source of love not give you what your heart truly desires when what it desires is the very essence of who I am? I am love. I know that you desire to be loved and cherished . . . outwardly and inwardly. I raise the dead. Can I not breathe life and passion into the human heart? Oh, you of little faith, believe that you have received that which you have asked for and wait patiently knowing that my timing is perfect. I give when the heart is completely ready to receive. This often happens through trial, tribulation, and dark nights of the soul. Do you trust me? Have I ever abandoned you? Know that my timing takes into account eternity where there is no time . . . only the present. Be present to me through this difficult time, and everything will take place in my timing for your ultimate good. To give to someone that which is not ready to be fully received is foolish. Embrace all of me in this trial and you will feel me embracing all of you. Love yourself.

AUGUST 30, 2005

"So Shadrach, Meshach and Abednego came out of the fire, and the satraps, prefects, governors and royal advisers crowded around them. They saw that the fire had not harmed their bodies, nor was a hair of their heads singed; their robes were not scorched, and there was no smell of fire on them" (Daniel 3:26–27).

"Why does your teacher eat with tax collectors and 'sinners'?" On hearing this, Jesus said, 'It is not the healthy who need a doctor, but the sick. But go and learn what this means: 'I desire mercy, not sacrifice.' For I have not come to call the righteous, but sinners" (Matthew 9:11–13).

Jesus: Let me carry you through your weakest moments. Remember Shadrach, Meshach, and Abednego? I met them in the fire. Did they not walk out of it without so much as one singed hair? I do the same for you. I am with you through each fire, trial, and struggle. I remain faithful even through your small acts of unfaithfulness. Has not your love and compassion for other souls in your life doubled with each personal act of falling down and each uplifting experience of reconciliation? You are growing in love . . . is that not what you have always asked of me? "Lord, make me a missionary of love?" The answers to your struggles lie within your own heart's desires . . . listen to your heart . . . the heart that you committed to me at seventeen. Increase your confidence in the truths that are deeply woven within the core of who you are. Remember the hand that wove them was pierced out of love for you . . . can you not trust in that love? Be still, surrender, embrace, and live out the truths that dwell in your heart. Follow your heart for it is fashioned after mine.

Take the time to be still before me. Have the courage to look deep inside the core of who you are . . . examine your thoughts and feelings without judgment . . . know yourself, love yourself. What moves you in life apart from others? What brings a smile to your face? What evokes laughter from your soul? What brings tears to your eyes or aching within your heart? What erupts anger within your soul? What makes you want to sing and dance in this world? What do you fear? What do you love? In order to love and know others you must first invest in loving and knowing yourself. You cannot give what you do not have. You cannot receive what you have not first received from yourself. Take time to know and love yourself. As I have said, you must love others as you love yourself. This will always lead to the profound intimacy in life that you are longing for . . . and freedom along with it!

SEPTEMBER 4, 2005

"They were glad when it grew calm and he guided them to their desired haven" (Psalm 107:30).

Me: I know now that you carry me to the exact spot in life where I am supposed to be, and when I can't move in that direction because I am paralyzed by pain, guilt, or shame, it is then that you pick me up and carry me there . . . into the promised land . . . the land that is truly flowing with milk and honey . . . our desired haven.

Jesus: Trust the truth that resides in your heart . . . be still and listen . . . all of the answers to your questions can be found within your heart.

SEPTEMBER 9, 2005
―――――――――――

"I consider that our present sufferings are not worth comparing with the glory that will be revealed in us" (Romans 8:18).

"For God did not give us a spirit of timidity, but a spirit of power, of love and of self-discipline" (2 Timothy 1:7).

Me: I am frustrated and anxious because of this traffic!

Jesus: Isn't it amazing how quickly the anxiety and frustration you experienced on your journey dissipated once you reached your destination? Use this experience to encourage your soul toward eternity. Trust that all of the fears, anxieties, and worries that you experience throughout your journey of life on earth will dissipate as soon as you reach your ultimate destination . . . eternal life in heaven. Know that all of these light and momentary struggles you are experiencing each day are achieving for you an eternal salvation that far outweighs them all. Let the truth of this give you strength to let go more and live out freely the music that has already been composed within your soul. Truly, I say to you, there is an eternal song that surrounds you daily that is not limited to any scale or note; its melody echoes an unlimited symphony of love and freedom throughout all of creation. Consider the lilies of the field, the birds of the air . . . no need for worry . . . for they allow themselves to be guided by the one who set their very existence into motion . . . enter into the freedom of unconditional love, for you are already engulfed in it . . . open your eyes to see it and your ears to hear it . . . for in it you live and move and have your being. Set yourself free from your internal prisons that you have built for yourself over time . . . they are based on lies rather than truth. You are beautifully and wonderfully created in love, for love, by love . . . this is your freedom, embrace it!

Sᴇᴘᴛᴇᴍʙᴇʀ 15, 2005

"Commit to the Lord whatever you do, and your plans will succeed" (Proverbs 16:3).

"'Lord, if it's you,' Peter replied, 'tell me to come to you on the water'" (Matthew 14:28).

"And we know that in all things God works for the good of those who love him, who have been called according to his purpose" (Romans 8:28).

Me: My beloved, here I am at a crossroads in my life . . . help me to know which road to travel on . . .

Jesus: All roads, my little one, when committed to me lead to life! Your choices often paralyze you. Your fear stems from the thought that you will make a wrong choice. Have you so little faith? Have you not heard that I make all things work together for an ultimate good? You cannot therefore, in your limited state as a human make a wrong decision about your future. Are some roads filled with more potholes, rocks, and turns than others? Yes, and my Father is able to work them all into a life of grace and love for those who are willing to be led along their road of choice.

The key to all crossroads in life is to commit each step to me along your way. Invite me into your decisions. Ask me to clear up your confusion. Ofttimes, it will come down to the step taken in faith . . . that one step of faith . . . the same one that Peter took when he stepped out of the boat onto the water. It is that first step that requires the most faith. Know that any step taken with faith will end in an ultimate good. Every experience and crossroad in life can then be looked at as an opportunity for growth and learning. Even when you feel the crushing power of the waves along your path, have confidence that your Jesus will always reach out to save you! Know that there is nothing that can happen in life that I will not give you the grace to be able to handle. Am I not your savior? Live in the confidence and freedom of this truth!

OCTOBER 25, 2005

"So they brought him. When the spirit saw Jesus, it immediately threw the boy into a convulsion. He fell to the ground and rolled around, foaming at the mouth. Jesus asked the boy's father, 'How long has he been like this?' 'From childhood,' he answered. 'It has often thrown him into fire or water to kill him. But if you can do anything, take pity on us and help us.' 'If you can?' said Jesus. 'Everything is possible for him who believes'" (Mark 9:20–23).

Me: Lord, it must be difficult for you to put up with our disbelief knowing that in one instant you can completely heal and restore. Truly, all things are possible for those who believe. I do believe . . . restore my life. Everything in all of creation is sustained and held together in your love. How is it possible then for us to doubt that you are capable of leading us into eternal life even through the deepest moments of despair and anguish, sadness, and grief? It is foolish then to ask. *If* you can help us . . . what can't you do? All things are possible with God! Forgive me for losing sight of your intimate presence in my life. I am separated now from my husband and I am fearful about my future and the peace inside the hearts of my three children.

Jesus: It is true, my little fearful one, all things are possible with me in you. Take heart and do not lose focus on the reality of my presence within you . . . my presence within the hearts of your children. Am I not the good, gentle shepherd? The father of the possessed son was filled with fear over the reality of his son's condition. He did not allow his fear to paralyze him; he allowed it to propel him into action. He felt his fear and went for a solution in spite of it. Even when faced with lifelong challenges do not cease in your conviction to find healing, love, peace, and life throughout your journey. It is the greatest storms in life that often produce the most radical acts of love and mercy within the human heart. Have confidence even when experiencing deep fear . . . I tell you again; Lauren, do not lose your confidence in the strength that resides within your soul when faced with fear! Push through it, knowing that all things are possible with God . . . all things. Know that you will be held close to my heart as we get to calm waters in your life. Do not be afraid . . . trust in your God . . . for he is able to carry you through your deepest fears . . . surrender and trust and you will see the wonders of God! Remember at the base of all fear is the thought that you will not be able to handle what comes your way and that you will not be okay. Know this, that with the strength of the one who created the universe dwelling within your being, you will have the strength to handle anything that comes your way! Remember this truth and live with confidence.

November 4, 2005

"I will instruct you and teach you in the way you should go; I will counsel you and watch over you. Do not be like the horse or the mule, which have no understanding but must be controlled by bit and bridle or they will not come to you" (Psalm 32:8–9).

Me: I feel lost and alone . . . why am I here? My divorce is going to be final on January 15!

Jesus: My child, rather than viewing the circumstances in life as forms of rejection, look at them as opportunities for direction. For it is through these defined moments of so called rejection or "dead ends" throughout your journey in life that you will find the guidance you are seeking. Look at every event, good or bad, as some form of guidance that is used to help you on your life journey. When you come to a dead end, you often still have the opportunity to go right or left. There is always another way that will be opened to you. Those dead ends are actually there to guide you on the path chosen for you to travel. Think of it as a maze . . . there is a definite path through it, yet you will encounter many obstacles before you find your way. The obstacles are simply a way to redirect you down another path . . . to one of deeper understanding, fuller love for yourself and others, stronger character, more persistent joy and peace, and profound faith and forgiveness.

January 10, 2006

"I will not die but live, and will proclaim what the Lord has done" (Psalm 118:17).

"The Lord will sustain him on his sickbed and restore him from his bed of illness" (Psalm 41:3).

Me: Father God, I am silenced within by the phone call I just received today that has changed my entire perception of my world in an instant . . . the words are still ringing in my ears. "Lauren, are you sitting down? We have the results of your biopsy . . . Lauren, you have cancer . . . Invasive Ductile Carcinoma grade three . . . and it's in your lymph nodes." I am shaking so hard I can barely write down my thoughts . . . I am only thirty-eight . . . my children . . . this must be someone else's diagnosis . . . they have the wrong person! I thought those lumps that I found were swollen lymph nodes from the flu . . . the doctor thought the same thing, even after seeing them on the ultrasound!! For once in my life, I am completely at a loss and devastated beyond what my pen can write. *Too much*! I am just finding my way through divorce after sixteen years of marriage! My children's faces flood my mind . . . everything within my being as I knew it is lost in the grief and disbelief that is now flooding my soul . . . I am paralyzed . . . I cannot think. Who am I? Where do I live? Are my feet touching the ground? I cannot see through the wall of tears . . . I can't breathe . . . Jesus, I have lost myself and my faith in one instant. I am frozen in time . . . everything is frozen in time around me . . . Jesus . . . I don't hear your voice within my heart yet a small voice in my head is speaking to me of your presence . . . I can feel nothing... I hear you speak that you will never leave me or forsake me... *Lord*, I feel left and forsaken! My God, My God... why have you forsaken me! Everything in my whole being is crying out against this! I am only thirty-eight! My fears are rendering me deaf and blind at this moment... this is beyond what I can bear... you *must* pick me up and carry me through every second of this... for I am not physically able to stand at this moment in my life. Did I pray too boldly over the years when I asked over and over to be used as a missionary of your love to the world? Were my bold prayers spoken out of pure ignorance of what I was asking? Know my weakness, Lord... I feel this is too much for me to bear! Save me from this experience in life... Lord, I am terrified ... I can't even remember your words of comfort that have been flowing through my heart and pen so easily over the years. *Everything* is silenced. I am consumed by fear and darkness. *Cancer*?! *No,* I refuse this sentence... *no*! I want to run like Jonah! I'm scared, Jesus... hold me... carry me ... you know who I am... deliver me from this if I cannot shine for you through it. At this point, I don't even want to shine... I had no preparation for this day as I can see it at this moment! Yes, I did my breast exams *every* month ... how can this be that it just "showed up" and it's already invasive and in my lymph nodes? What is the purpose of this now? Speak to me clearly, slowly, and with great tenderness, Lord... for your little flower has been crushed, yet I know deep within my being that by your grace I will not be destroyed by this. I am like a little child... take my trembling hand, Jesus, and lead my broken heart that is filled with fear on through the darkness that is blinding me at this moment in time... my tears are endless. I am blind and deaf, yet my heart is open to be led. I am so emotional about the phone call I just made to my mom . . . she was waiting for these results. I heard her voice and could not speak.

"Lauren, is that you?" Again, fear, and shock had stolen my voice . . . yet because of the strong heart connection that I share with my family, my mom replied to the silence, "I will be there tomorrow Lauren." And I hung up. She was at my house in less than twenty-four hours all the way from New York City. This makes me weep . . . my tears are mixed with my mom's love for me and fear all at the same time.

Jesus: You are about to witness love in action more than ever before in your life. Be still . . . know . . . that I . . . AM God!

Over 12 robins filled a tree outside my window one morning after a snowstorm.

Before my hair fell out I gave it away to Locks of Love. They sectioned it off into what seemed like over 100 little pony tails before cutting each one off.

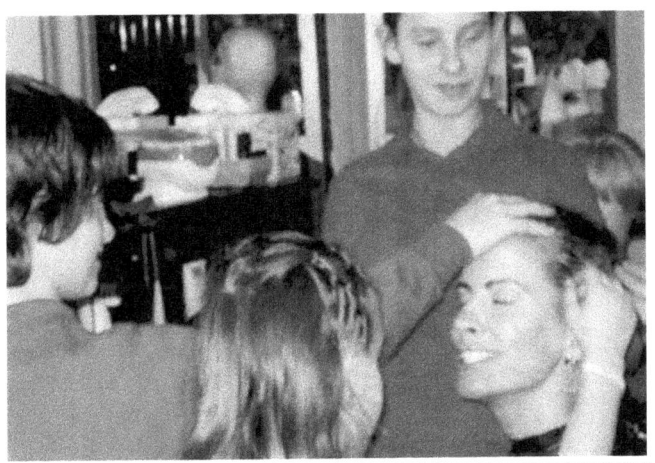

My children's reaction to the experience of giving my hair away.

My Dad is wearing my hair so I could style the back of it for my cousins wedding. I danced so hard that night that my hair fell off . . . literally.

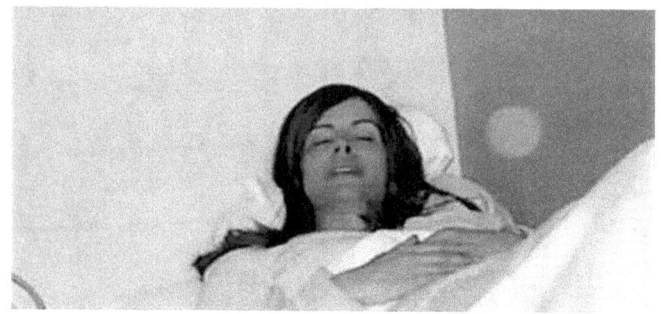
In the hospital after a chemo infusion.

A photo taken during a contemplative moment before the mastectomy.

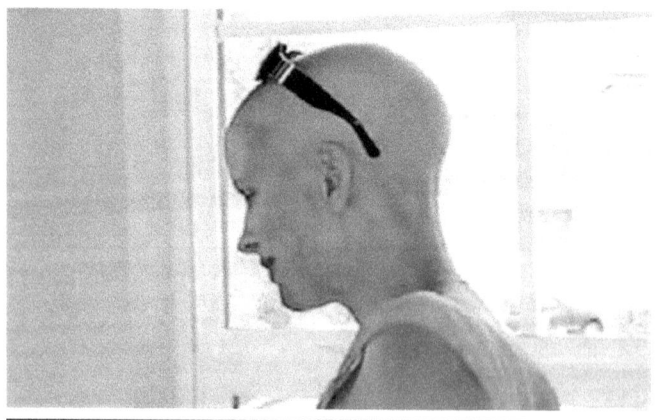
My summer hairdo.

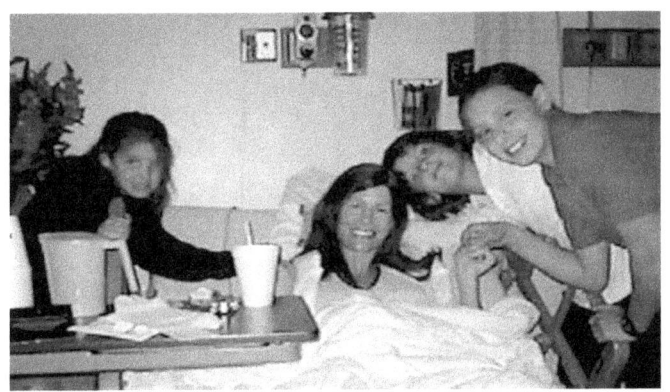

After my mastectomy in the hospital with my children.

My friend Susan and I a few months before she died.

DURING

January 20, 2006

"The one who calls you is faithful and he will do it"
(1 Thessalonians 5:24).

Me: I am denial . . . Lord. I am being told that I need chemo for three months followed by surgery . . . a double mastectomy . . . more chemo and possible radiation. I see this genderless person standing in my imagination, and I am so scared! No hair, no breasts and I am forced to look deeply into the message I have preached to others over the last twenty years . . . beauty flows from the heart, man looks at the outer appearance and God looks at the heart. Can I take ownership for all of the words and truths you have revealed to my soul over the years? Do I believe? I stand silenced before you, Jesus . . . lead me by the heart through this storm deep in the silence of my soul I say to you . . . Lord, help my unbelief, help my unbelief. I desire to walk on top of the tumultuous waters, yet I sit frozen with fear in the boat . . . fill my trembling soul with courage to step out of this boat . . . keeping my eyes fixed on you knowing that you are my divine physician . . . renew my faith . . . reach out your hand, that was pierced out of love for me and save me once again. More deeply than ever I cry out to you! Hear my cry, oh Lord, and rescue your little child from this storm! I want out!

Jesus: My precious little one . . . remember who you are . . . you are my beloved one . . . recall how often you have asked me to be a little flower with a huge fragrance of love, compassion, and mercy to the world . . . I can assure you all of your prayers have been answered, and I have already won victory for you over all that you feel paralyzed by now at this moment of trial. Remember my words and believe . . . I, the Lord almighty, the divine physician will fight your battle . . . you have only to be still . . . for it is not in the great storm that you hear my voice . . . no, it is in the quiet whispers that echo within the heart of faith. Stand firm, my little warrior . . . be still and know that I am your God . . . Abba . . . Father . . . nothing is impossible for me. Nothing is impossible for you for I have instilled within you at the moment of your conception a spirit of power, strength and courage. That is why I say to you, Lauren . . . remember who you are! Remember that anything that comes against you will not prevail . . . your soul belongs to me and the battle has already been won! You already have victory over this . . . I call you out by name to embrace it! You are my beloved one and nothing shall prevail against that! Be still and listen for my voice in the silence of your heart. I will speak to you even throughout the darkest nights. Has darkness ever consumed the light? Even the smallest flame will always swallow up the night. You are a child of the light . . . an endless burning flame of love that will shine throughout all eternity . . . remember who you are!

February 9, 2006

"To keep me from becoming conceited because of these surpassingly great revelations, there was given me a thorn in my flesh, a messenger of Satan, to torment me. Three times I pleaded with the Lord to take it away from me. But he said to me, 'My grace is sufficient for you, for my power is made perfect in weakness.' Therefore I will boast all the more gladly about my weaknesses, so that Christ's power may rest on me. That is why, for Christ's sake, I delight in weaknesses, in insults, in hardships, in persecutions, in difficulties. For when I am weak, then I am strong" (2 Corinthians 12:7–10).

Me: Lord, I am just one week past my first chemo treatment. I don't really remember much of the first five days after my treatment. I'm tired and worn down . . . speak, Lord . . . your servant is listening. I am told that I will be bald in fourteen days. My hair is now half way down my back. I don't want to be bald! I am scared to see myself bald . . . *no*! I don't want this! *No*!

Jesus: My little flower . . . my love for you is complete and unconditional. I want to speak to you about the purification of the soul. Until you are true and real with yourself . . . honest with the place that you are within your soul, you will continue to feel blocks within your being that will leave you frustrated and unclear in your identity. You must be willing to experience all of your emotions at this time . . . give yourself freedom to be real.

Me: What does that look like for me? I don't even know who I am right now!

Jesus: Lauren, my sweet child of love, you have fought so hard in your life to be seen as "good" . . . always doing the "right thing." Rather than striving so hard in the direction of perfection, it is my desire for you that you grow in the freedom of seeing yourself as fully loved just as you are, right where you are . . . within the realm of all of your emotions, feelings, and passions. It is there, in that place, that you will experience the depth of true life and love that I came and died to offer to you. Grab a hold of all that you are . . . without shame or guilt . . . you are beautiful to me . . . just as you are. You are holding back with yourself . . . feeling guilty for having thoughts that you deem "negative" or "unholy" in that they lack faith or trust. Truly, I say unto you . . . I have come to meet you in every thought and emotion to lead you into the experience of being alive in me . . . unashamed and truly confident of the person you are . . . I want you to experience with confidence and freedom every emotion that arises within your heart without judgment as it comes to you through this trial. For it is in this experience and the permission that you give yourself to be "real" through it all that will ultimately render the emotions of fear, doubt, anxiety, anger, and grief . . . powerless over you. In giving yourself permission to fully experience all emotions you ultimately free yourself from being controlled by them and your confidence in the beautiful person you are will become your true identity.

February 13, 2006

"The thief comes to kill and destroy. I have come that you may have life and have it to the full" (John 10:10).

Me: Today, as I lie in my bed, I am feeling a deep sense of peace and love surrounding me . . . I realize as I gaze around my room that I have surrounded myself with those things that bring peace and comfort to my heart . . . cards from friends, flowers, pictures of my family, my favorite books, crosses, my journal, and beautiful music. I have created a place of refuge for myself, with the help of my mom and dad, sister, family, and friends, a place of safety where I can allow myself to simply be. I am safe here to experience any and every emotion that wells up in my body. Today, I feel at peace. I'm allowing your love that you have showered on me through my children, family, friends, and strangers to flood my soul and sustain me in a place of serenity and calm. I am beginning to truly believe that I am beautiful . . . that I am loved . . . that I have everything I need within me to rise above this condition of cancer and live fully . . . I am feeling that it is a new birth for me. You are allowing me to see myself through this experience as you see me Father . . . beautifully and wonderfully created to be known and to know, to love and to be loved. It's funny, all of these years I have been writing about this great love and it is only now, having the experience of cancer, that the eyes of my heart are truly opening to the reality that I truly am loved and beautiful . . . not because of my looks on the outside, but because of the beauty that lies within my soul . . . a beauty so dignified, feminine, romantic, alluring, and sensual it could never be fully expressed through any physical form.

Therefore, anything that may change or be taken away physically about me during this time will not touch who I truly am as a woman of God. My true beauty will always remain untouched. Oh, Jesus, please help me to remember this peaceful moment of truth when I begin to weep and grieve over the loss of my hair and breasts . . . I know that day will come! I never thought I attached any of my identity to my physical self. I have been blessed with natural beauty physically, and yet I thought I had my priorities right, knowing that my true beauty comes from my soul not from my external looks. I am now challenged deeply within my being. I know that because of so many moments of fear and grief I am experiencing over the upcoming loss of my beautiful long brown hair and breasts that I have attached some of my identity to them. Thank you, God, for the opportunity to experience being beautiful, truly beautiful, without those physical representations of what I attached part of my identity to . . . how freeing this will be . . . this too shall pass and when my hair grows back, and the doctors have reconstructed my breasts, I will know that my beauty truly shines from my soul out. I pray that nothing will ever be able to threaten that truth again . . . age or illness . . . my beautiful soul will remain untouched! Thank you for this moment Lord! Even though my body and mind are very fuzzy because of the chemo, my spirit is very strong, and I am dancing through this storm. Even though I am lying in fetal position and my body is trembling because of the poison, I see myself dancing on a hill in a white dress . . . this is a crazy experience!

Jesus: Once you are through this experience, my child, I assure you that you will never question your beauty again . . . and no one and no thing on earth will ever be able to steal that away from you.

FEBRUARY 14, 2006

"During the fourth watch of the night Jesus went out to them, walking on the lake. When the disciples saw him walking on the lake, they were terrified. 'It's a ghost,' they said, and cried out in fear. But Jesus immediately said to them: 'Take courage! It is I. Don't be afraid.' 'Lord, if it's you,' Peter replied, 'tell me to come to you on the water.' 'Come,' he said. Then Peter got down out of the boat and walked on the water to Jesus. But when he saw the wind, he was afraid and beginning to sink, he cried out, 'Lord, save me!' Immediately Jesus reached out his hand and caught him. ' ou of little faith,' he said, 'why did you doubt?'" (Matthew 14:25–31).

Me: Today, I am losing my long, half way down my back, beautiful brown hair! I woke up this morning, Lord, so thankful as I reached up as I have been doing every morning for the last three weeks and gently tugged on my hair, relieved that not one strand came out. I was hopeful the chemo had left my roots in tact after only one dose. Three hours later, I repeated the same "hair check" routine and this time I ended up with about fifteen hairs in my hand. I continued to tug and pull at little pieces . . . all of which easily came out of my head into my hand. At first, I was amazed at the ease at which they fell out of my head so I began to make a little pile of hair on the counter. I stood before this little pile in shock that my hair was actually falling out on the fourteenth day after my first day of chemo . . . the doctors where right on target. It is the fourteenth day today . . . Valentine's Day. I broke down sobbing uncontrollably . . . holding the little pile of hair in my hands . . . experiencing a deep sense of loss. I am grieving, Lord! Like I am letting go of a part of me that is dying! I will cut it off and give it away to Locks of Love this afternoon, Lord, before I don't have enough left to give away. This will give some purpose to the pain I feel inside. My sister says that she can deal with a bald sister, but she can't deal with a dead sister. I love my sister . . . she dropped everything many times already to fly out and be by my side . . . more than ever in my life, God . . . I love my sister! I am fighting, God, for not only myself but for my whole family and my children. I hear that and yet I am grieving over this loss . . . deeply . . . carry me through this day, Lord . . . once again I have fallen to the floor . . . pick me up . . . breathe your life into me once again . . . not once have you forsaken me through this . . . I am broken and crushed in spirit and I believe in your healing touch. I know I have found favor with you!

Later in the day, after giving away my hair:
Lord, I cried so hard today after getting my hair cut off. I need to write down everything that moved my heart about this experience. I have about a half an inch of hair left on my head. I was able to donate over ten inches of my hair to Locks of Love...they will make one nice wig from it. I keep saying that to try to give a little extra purpose to my pain. My three children and my mom came with me today. First, the hairdresser tied off little sections of my hair and put them into rubber bands. By the time I was finished my whole head was covered with about 50 sections of hair. I'm sure enough to make three wigs! Then the cutting began. She cut off one section of hair at a time right above each rubber band, leaving behind about a half an inch of hair on my head. I looked in the mirror and watched the process . . . so many emotions were traveling through my body . . .

but all I was capable of at that point was simple observation. I looked in the mirror after she cut off the last section and quickly looked away and tried to make some kind of joke, but inside I was losing it fast. My children's little hands kept touching my head as they looked at me with wide eyes. My youngest said, "Mommy is that still you?" I thought to myself for a split second, *I don't know*. But, I assured her it was me. I wanted to run and hide but felt I needed to be strong for my kids. Then the wig went on and the styling began in a desperate attempt to make it look as much like my hair as possible.

My son seemed very distressed as he continually said, "It's too bulky, Mom; it doesn't look like you." My feelings and emotions started to well up so strongly within my body that I felt like disappearing, running away, and hiding until this is all over. But, I remained for my children's sake . . . I remained.

My mom drove us all home. About two minutes after leaving I took the wig off and felt the tears welling up beyond my ability to control. My mom picked up on this and said, "Let it flow, Lauren, let it flow. It's good for you and your kids to be real." So I did . . . I let it flow and flow and flow and flow and flow. The sobs continued on and off for hours. My children were now comforting me with words that I have used to comfort them over the years.

"Mom, let it all out, it's not good to hold it in".

"Mom, tell me everything you are feeling right now."

"Mom, look at this like grass. They mowed it down and it will grow back." I found it very interesting as I shared my grief to see my son's whole attitude change from one of panic over not getting a wig that looks just like me to one of confidence that hair doesn't matter. "It's not the hair that makes you beautiful, Mom; it's your soul and your face. You look like the woman in the James Bond movie . . . and besides, don't worry because your soul has hair . . . long beautiful hair." All of these statements and words of comfort that flowed from my beautiful children's hearts all helped my heart start to see a little ray of light in this dark moment . . . light and perspective.

I came in the house and my mom said, "Why don't you go on upstairs and spend some time alone." I couldn't even respond but nodded my head and slowly made my way to my room . . . I was actually relieved to be alone with you, Jesus . . . alone to be me at this moment in time. I looked forward to entering my little place of safety and refuge that I had created for myself over the past weeks of my experience with cancer. However, the moment my body passed through the door, I collapsed on the floor and the sobbing began. I wept so hard and deeply that I didn't recognize myself. I kept saying over and over, "I want my long hair back . . . I don't recognize myself in the mirror." The last time my hair was this short was the day I was born. There has to be some kind of message in that thought . . . maybe this is symbolic for a rebirth in my soul that I am experiencing . . . a rebirth into a new freedom. I was too weak to explore that thought. I was snapped out of my sobs as the door opened and my sweet son walked in and sat on the floor next to me. I saw fear in his big blue eyes, "Johnny, I want you to know that I'm not crying because I'm going to die or even because I have cancer right now. I'm not going to die, and I will overcome this cancer . . . I'm crying because I miss my long hair, and God asks us to share everything with him that hurts our heart in any way." He seemed relieved. He sat there for a while rubbing my back and looking into my eyes then he spoke, "Mom, look at that picture of Jesus on your desk; they stripped him naked and beat him and killed him, and he came back from the dead stronger than ever . . . even his skin looked good." Those words pierced my heart and sank deep into places within my soul I never knew existed before this moment . . . I was filled with a sense of joy and gratitude knowing my son got it . . . he got it. The message that I have preached for so many years was a truth to my sweet son. Lord, there is a greater good in all of this . . . not just one good but many "goods" that are coming from this trial and I am so thankful that I am able to see them through my pain.

I got up and laid on my bed, Johnny picked up the book, *The Velveteen Rabbit,* by Margery Williams that we had been reading together. Each word he read hit me as if God had opened the heavens and poured healing waters straight into my wounded heart. God, you spoke the truths I needed to hear at that moment in time through the mouth of a child and through the words of a children's book. "At that time Jesus said, 'I praise you, Father, Lord of heaven and earth, because you have hidden these things from the wise and learned, and revealed them to little children. Yes, Father, for this was your good pleasure" (Matthew 11:25–26). How blessed I was at that moment to witness the truth of your words, Lord, my precious savior. As my son began to read the following words, it was revealed to my soul with complete clarity the true essence of beauty in its simplest form.

"What is Real?" asked the Rabbit one day, when they were lying side by side near the nursery fender . . .

"Real isn't how you are made," said the Skin Horse. "It's a thing that happens to you when a child loves you for a long, long time, not just to play with, but really loves you, then you become Real." . . .

"Does it hurt?" asked the Rabbit.

"Sometimes," said the Skin Horse, for he was always truthful. "When you are Real you don't mind being hurt."

"Does it happen all at once, like being wound up," he asked, "or bit by bit?"

"It doesn't happen all at once," said the Skin Horse. "You become. It takes a long time. That's why it doesn't often happen to people who break easily or have sharp edges, or who have to be carefully kept. Generally, by the time you are Real, most of your hair has been loved off, your eyes drop out and you get loose in the joints and very shabby. But these things don't matter at all, because once you are Real you can't be ugly, except to people who don't understand."

. . . weeks passed, and the little Rabbit grew very old and shabby, but the boy loved him just as much. He loved him so hard that he loved all his whiskers off, and the pink lining to his ears turned gray, and his brown spots faded. He even began to lose his shape, and he scarcely looked like a rabbit any more, except to the Boy. To him he was always beautiful, and that was all that the little Rabbit cared about. He didn't mind how he looked to other people, because the nursery magic had made him Real, and when you are Real shabbiness doesn't matter.[1]

"Mom, you're the rabbit!" my son suddenly proclaimed, "See it doesn't matter if your hair falls out . . . you are loved and beautiful . . . I think you are beautiful." My tears started flowing again, but this time from a different place within. Rather than a place of grief and sadness, they flowed from a place of unspeakable gratitude and hope. I sat in awe of the deep truths that were flowing out of my son's little heart directly into mine . . . these were words of healing and peace . . . from this moment on I will never be the same again. I embraced my sweet boy and told him that he was being just like Jesus to me. For this moment alone . . . this is all worth it!

I got up . . . went into my bathroom, dried my face, put a little gel in my hair and a little gloss on my lips . . . as I looked in the mirror I said, "Lord, thank you that I am loved so much that I am becoming very *real* . . . for the first time in my life . . . I am experiencing what it means to be real." I walked downstairs. After a long intensive stare from my youngest daughter, she proclaimed, "Mom, you look like a neighbor." I burst into laughter and assured her I was not a neighbor that this is my home, I am her mom and even though my hair is gone I am still me.

Thank you, God, for these moments of truth today . . . these moments of profound love and truth! Truly, I know deep inside that I am more than okay with my hair falling out because I am so loved! This experience is so traumatic to me, and yet I know I need to go through this to become fully alive, completely real, and deeply aware that I am unconditionally loved. Thank you for carrying me to a place of peace and hope once again.

Jesus: Increase your confidence, my beautiful fragrant flower . . . do not allow for one minute your faith to waver . . . have I not continuously delivered you from the fowlers snares in life? This cancer shall not prevail against you . . . this too shall be overcome through your faith in my healing touch . . . all the while bringing you into the awareness that the very essence of your beauty flows from your soul out through your flesh. What does it matter then what may come against your flesh in your lifetime except that all physical ailments or stumbling blocks be used to solidify that true beauty flows from the heart . . . this truth has been validated to you again and again. Your true beauty flows from the great love that I have placed in your heart and it is to be used to draw others into love. I will engulf them with an unconditional love that will eventually blind them to the useless devices that once captivated their hearts and robbed them of true freedom and life. So shine, Lauren, shine through the loss of your physical appearance for a time knowing that you are gaining in the area of the eternal . . . shine knowing that this momentary trial is achieving for you an eternal glory and freedom from the things that you have attached your beauty to that far outweighs it all . . . know that your joy and sense of beauty will double within your soul as you learn to let go and trust. Remember you are my beloved child . . . you are constantly radiating with beauty. See yourself as I see you!

FEBRUARY 17, 2006

"You know when I sit and when I rise; you perceive my thoughts from afar. You discern my going out and my lying down; you are familiar with all my ways. Before a word is on my tongue you know it completely, O Lord . . . For you created my inmost being; you knit me together in my mother's womb. I praise you because I am fearfully and wonderfully made; your works are wonderful, I know that full well. My frame was not hidden from you when I was made in the secret place. When I was woven together in the depths of the earth, your eyes saw my unformed body. All the days ordained for me were written in your book before one of them came to be" (Psalm 139: 2–4; 13–16).

Me: Lord, I have spent the night focusing on the healing power of your light and love. It has come to my attention that I have not looked upon every fiber, every cell of who I am physically with great love. I have been allowing anger, resentment and grief to swallow up any intentions that are aimed at self-love and healing since my diagnosis of cancer. I have been thinking throughout the night that until I am able to allow your healing light and love to penetrate every cell in my body my faith in healing will be paralyzed by my fears. I want to wake up from my slumber and allow you to resurrect your healing presence within my whole being. Today, I am choosing to love and I will allow myself to be loved. This is my intention. I can see in my mind all of the little cells in my body, and I choose to nurture and love every cell that I see is moving about in the wholeness of love and health. However, every cell that is bent on destruction and death rather than life has no place in this body of mine. I release within my body at this moment the intention to guide the gift of this chemotherapy to those cells that are bent on destruction. I command it to go specifically to those cells that are bent on destruction. I command it to go specifically to those sick cells and destroy them forever. After they are removed from my body, I am imagining every healthy cell that is surrounded with your love and filled with faith in life to replace and protect every sight of victory within my body. As this chemo, which I am choosing to see as a gift, floods my system, I am choosing to keep its negative effects away from other parts of my body deep within me that may be injured by it. May every healthy cell, guided by your love and protection, stand guard to protect me. I love every fiber and cell, my heavenly Father, which you so carefully knit together in my mother's womb. I claim victory over these intruding cells that are fooled to think they will have their way with me! I am feeling very strong this morning, and I rise out of my bed to give you all thanks and praise for giving me this beautiful body that also has the ability and has always had the ability to heal and protect itself. I am so excited to see the full potential of this truth that you have been revealing to my soul throughout the night! I choose this day to love myself as you love me . . . without criticism or judgment but as one who is constantly bathed in the healing power for your unconditional love! I feel born anew today!

Jesus: My child, as I revealed earlier my intention is that you remember who you are . . . I rejoice in the truths that you are opening yourself up to see . . . you have had these beautiful treasures within you since the moment you were conceived. What a joy it is for me to see you discovering these gifts that have remained unopened throughout your short life! There are many more to come my beautiful one . . . many more to be discovered and embraced. You have only begun to discover all of the beautiful jewels of life that are embedded in the woman I created you to be! Continue to seek, ask, and knock!

Me: I wait in eager expectation my beloved divine physician!

FEBRUARY 25, 2006

"For God, who said, 'Let light shine out of darkness,' made his light shine in our hearts to give us the light of the knowledge of the glory of God in the face of Christ. But we have this treasure in jars of clay to show that this all-surpassing power is from God and not from us. We are hard pressed on every side, but not crushed; perplexed, but not in despair; persecuted, but not abandoned; struck down, but not destroyed" (Corinthians 4:6–9).

Me: Round II of chemo . . . *wow* this one knocked me down harder than the first . . . I'm having a flash back to when I was in the State Championship for Tae Kwon Do and this lady kicked me in the head and I was knocked to the floor. I remember hearing the count, and when the referee got to about five, I told myself that I had not trained six days a week, four hours a day to go out like this so I got up and beat her . . . I ended up with the silver medal, and I was happy with that . . . I am pulling from every moment of victory in my life right now! Yes . . . no doubt, Lord . . . I am knocked down, and I will get up before anyone can count to ten . . . every day I have many opportunities to begin again.

As I am laying here in my bed, I am aware of how much I strive in my soul . . . I'm striving to make sense of all of this . . . striving to figure out ways to inspire the world by this experience . . . striving to rise above the effects of chemo . . . to reach a higher level of spiritual consciousness so I can provide the right environment for my body to heal itself . . . Lord you have said that you have already given me everything I need for life and godliness . . . I continue to hear Your voice echo within my soul saying to the depth of who

I am, "Daughter, your faith has healed you" (Mark 5:34). I hear all of this and then something pulls at me . . . deep at my core . . . a small voice that keeps getting louder, "Too much striving . . . let go and just be . . . let go and let God." This is a crash course titled: Who is Lauren 101 . . . and what makes her tick. I strive . . . strive . . . strive . . . definitely more of a Martha type than a Mary. I want to be more like Mary . . . I desire to feel at peace, listening, sitting, and being. Help me to be still so that I can know what it is like to allow my life to unfold before me rather than desperately striving to unwrap it all! My mom said that I ripped the nipple off my bottle when I was very young because the milk wasn't coming out fast enough for me.

Jesus: Contemplate the rose for a moment . . . the fullness of its fragrance and beauty is patiently contained within. It is content to allow the hand of its maker to gently unfold its pedals . . . its essence and purpose revealed through surrender and trust over time . . . never doubting for a moment that all it was created for will reach completion!

MARCH 3, 2006

"I run in the path of your commands, for you have set my heart free . . . I will walk about in freedom, for I have sought out your precepts" (Psalm 119: 32, 45).

Me: This is my message through this experience to date. "Remember who I am." Speak the truth that makes up who I am . . . first to myself . . . acknowledge it, accept it, and own it. Then be transparent before God . . . don't pretend, don't say what I think I should say, what I think others want me to say, or what will protect me from criticism or rejection. Speak my truth as God has revealed who I truly am to my heart. Be who I am . . . before me, before God . . . real, honest, open. Then, very importantly, speak these revealed truths to the world in love, not out of ego, anger or fear, but in love . . . accepting and loving others as they share their truths and self just as they are, right where they are . . . and if they are still hiding their true selves behind fears, anger, rejection, or pain, I want to increase the love all the more. Love always overcomes, always penetrates beyond the flesh into the soul. I desire to offer it generously knowing that I have been saved by love, for love, to love. It is love that is healing, restoring, and setting me free, and it is the gift of love that I will offer the world until the last breath I take on this planet in the hopes of freeing others to simply be who they are from a place of love rather than judgment. To be all they were created to be ... real, uncensored, and free ... and most importantly aware of how loved they are, right where they are. I desire that I can say with confidence to the world as Jesus said in Matthew 14:27 with confidence to those who were afraid, "Take Courage! It is I. Don't be afraid." Jesus, you were never afraid of revealing who you were, who you are. May I have the grace to live in that kind of freedom without fear but aware only of love given and received from God, others and myself … is that not the very purpose for which I was born? Do not be afraid … it is Lauren.

Jesus: Wake up, oh, sleeper, and rise from the dead! The full essence of the woman you were created to be is drawing near!

April 16, 2006 (Easter)

"Therefore, since we have a great high priest who has gone through the heavens, Jesus the Son of God, let us hold firmly to the faith we profess. For we do not have a high priest who is unable to sympathize with our weaknesses, but we have one who has been tempted in every way, just as we are—yet was without sin. Let us then approach the throne of grace with confidence, so that we may receive mercy and find grace to help us in our time of need" (Hebrews 4:14–16).

Me: Yes, Lord, you are my great high priest, and you are able to sympathize with my weakness and trial. I am definitely not one to shrink back and be destroyed by anything in life! Today, I claim the power of the Holy Spirit within me who cries out to the truth that I will overcome all that is coming against me in my life! I claim the power of your Spirit within me . . . the same power that raised you from the dead. Holy Spirit rise up within my weak body, strengthen my legs and arms to go forth into this world and proclaim the faithful love of my Savior. Today, I am renewing my commitment to witness your love to the ends of the world . . . you can handle the details. I am yours . . . I am in love with you. I understand that you are my atoning sacrifice that has set me free . . . no more is needed except my open hands and heart. Thank you that you are able to save me completely not half way! You live to intercede for me, to carry me . . . to hold me close to your heart . . . to fill my heart and life with joy in my Spirit. Empower me to rise up and walk on top of the tumultuous waters that surround me or give me the skill and strength to ride the waves!

Jesus: You are my little flower meant to exude the fragrance of my love to the world. Open your hands and heart and I will fill them with an abundance of love so great that your suffering will be swallowed up in it! It will not haunt you anymore . . . forever it will be consumed by the furnace of my eternal love for you. You are strong today, Lauren; this is the day you remember my earthly death . . . do not be surprised that I am filling you with strength and love . . . it is a gift to remind you that it is in dying (in suffering, pain, and discomfort) that the most abundant new life, strength, purpose, conviction, and freedom to love God, others, and yourself will burst forth in you . . . consuming your soul, running over into every aspect of your life! Swim in it, Lauren . . . I have set you free today to run and not grow weary, walk and not grow faint. Dance this day in the freedom of my radically unlimited love! It was offered up for you . . . here is your life before you . . . breathe it into every part of your being then run free, like that wild horse you admire, and take this message to the ends of the world!

Me: My heart beats with anticipation knowing that all of this suffering has a purpose that is much bigger than I will ever be able to grasp . . . I tremble with excitement knowing that you are my dance partner, Jesus . . . you will teach me every step that I need to know. This dance will captivate and inspire the world . . . multitudes will want to enter in . . . lead me on, Lord . . . lead me on. All things work together for an ultimate good with you in me.

Keep me safe through my double mastectomy; I know my dance is not over . . . it's only just begun. This is my final death physically speaking . . . they will not take anything else from me. I have lost all my hair, my strength, and now my breasts . . . it is time to rebuild, reclaim, and rejuvenate all that I have lost through this . . . Lord it is time for new birth and new life and to focus on what I have gained. It's interesting to me when I walk around bald how people respond . . . my baldness seems to unleash compassion and kindness in the hearts of people I encounter . . . it's a very beautiful opportunity to give and receive love. After surgery on Monday, I will have hit rock bottom . . . it's all uphill for me! I am ready to embrace the abundant life that you have in store for me. You are faithful! Bring it on!

MAY 10, 2006

"Consider it pure joy, my brothers, whenever you face trials of many kinds, because you know that the testing of your faith develops perseverance. Perseverance must finish its work so that you may be mature and complete, not lacking anything" (James 1:2–4).

Me: Lord, I trust that through all of this you will guide me to my desired haven. I have read many things about cancer and that I will now be at a higher risk for other cancers. Once again, I am faced with the choice to trust you in this or to give in to fear. After the trials you have carried me through this far, I have learned to say, "Where else do I go but to you." For me, there is no other choice but you in this. Cast out all fear within me and renew my confidence within my soul. My life is for you, created by you . . . in you I live and walk and have my being. Each morning you fill my lungs and soul with the breath of life. One day at a time Lord, give to me my daily bread.

I have been able to sum up my cancer experience into a four phase cycle that I will work through sometimes several times a week: suffering, love, surrender, and finally freedom.

My suffering can take many different forms depending on the treatments that I am receiving as well as my mental and spiritual state. Emotionally my suffering has included anger, fear, rejection, grief, severe anxiety, crying, loneliness, confusion, depression, frustration, impatience, and humility. Physically my suffering has included body chills, body aches, muscle pain, nerve pain, hair loss, impaired thinking and reasoning (lack of ability to read and write), numbness in limbs, loss of my breasts, nausea, loss of appetite, loss of taste, injections, loss of consciousness, and fatigue. Spiritually, my suffering has included doubt, lack of faith, anger toward God, severe spiritual darkness, unanswered prayers, feelings of separation from God, confusion about my beliefs, lack of trust, and fear of suffering itself . . . overall, dark nights of the soul.

From all of this suffering there is one thing that has continually brought me out of each suffering experience and that is your reckless pursuit of my heart. Your love, Lord, has continued to reach down into the deepest parts of my suffering experiences and restore my soul, my emotional state and my physical being. No matter how low or how deep in despair I have found myself through this trial of cancer and divorce, it is your love that has continually saved me from a state of hopelessness. In spite of the intense moments of suffering, the love I have experienced through this has transformed me and continues to transform me into a woman of conviction, freedom and love that continues to radiate through my entire life experience. My entire family is amazing. My mom has moved in with me, my dad comes on weekends, my sister comes often, my brothers continue to support me, and my friends continue to make meals, drive me to the hospital, cry with me, hold me, love me . . . talk about a reason to live! My children . . . my three beautiful children . . . I have no words to describe the depth of feeling I have within my being that could capture the deep love and gratitude I have for the joy and love they fill my life with daily. My oldest daughter continues to light candles in my room and turn on my music at night. Truly, she has the heart of an angel.

This unlimited reckless pursuit for my heart has continually left me in a state of complete surrender again and again . . . and awe at the power of love in action. It is a kind of surrender that I have never experienced in my life until now. It does not mean giving up by any means, rather this surrender has evoked a profound sense of trust and letting go of all that causes anxiety and worry within my entire being. Like love, Lord, it too is reckless and unlimited. It flows from a deep realization that I am completely out of control of my life situation and in a state of helplessness when it comes to my next breath. I believe that if you were to stop thinking of me for one second, I would cease to exist. Other than for my choice to choose you and your promises to carry me through this cancer experience and been completely out of my control. What I have learned through this is that it has taken cancer to wake me up to the truth that with or without cancer . . . my life, my breath, the length of my days on earth are all ultimately out of my control . . . now what does this realization lead me to? *Freedom*! This is the final phase and destination of my soul in all of this . . . emotionally, spiritually, and physically. Lord, you are leading me into a freedom to *be* and to *live* just as I am, not because of anything I accomplish or achieve or any way I dress or physically look in this world . . . no, I am free from all of this again and again because through the pain, I have eyes to see that I am beautiful and loved and surrounded continually by your presence through all of this and the plans you have for me are ultimately achieving a deep sense of who I am . . . a beautiful woman with a spirit of perseverance, strength, and character that is here on earth as long as you want me to love and be loved for your honor and glory . . . to spread the beautiful fragrance of your love to the ends of the world in every area of my life and in the lives of those you have entrusted to me.

Jesus: You are beautiful to me, my small flower of love. All of my children are beautiful to me; they end up in despair and sadness when they lose sight of their true identity. Your life experiences on earth will include suffering of many kinds and dimensions. Truly, I have told you before, in this world you will have these trials but take heart, I have overcome the world! Live for the infinite, not for the finite. Set your heart on love, for it is eternal and is not diminished by suffering. Rather, it is deepened and strengthened through it! As you are discovering, suffering leads to true freedom within. It is for freedom that I have set you free. Stand firm in the truths you are learning through this trial and do not allow yourself to be burdened again by the yoke of slavery to fear. Remember that perfect love holds your very being together. Swim in it . . . venture out into the deep waters of my love . . . it is endless and it will always consume and destroy all fear.

MAY 17, 2006

"Therefore we do not lose heart. Though outwardly we are wasting away, yet inwardly we are being renewed day by day. For our light and momentary troubles are achieving for us an eternal glory that far outweighs them all. So we fix our eyes not on what is seen, but on what is unseen. For what is seen is temporary, but what is unseen is eternal" (2 Corinthians 4:16–18).

Me: So after my mastectomy, I had my mom cover all of my mirrors. Why? Because I wasn't ready to look at myself bald and breast less . . . I have learned to accept myself right where I am without judgment. My mom said that some cultures don't even have mirrors because they believe that the image in the mirror masks their true beauty. I believe that. When I did finally get the courage to look at myself, I didn't recognize me. I sat in silence as I slowly surveyed the damage done by the cancer. When I finally pulled my gaze away from the scars on my blank chest, I got very close to the mirror and looked into my eyes . . . there I was, for a minute I thought I lost myself . . . but there I was looking back at me . . . this is crazy . . . I know it's me in there, but I don't recognize anything physical about me . . . no hair, no breasts . . . it's amazing how those two things define women in our society: hair and breasts . . . in light of that definition, what am I? I don't think I have ever looked into my own eyes before . . . I was always checking out my other parts to see if they looked good enough to go out into the world . . . I don't think I have ever truly seen into me before . . . I have heard that the eyes are the window to the soul but I have never experienced the profound truth of this statement until this very moment in time. As I peered through my ransacked earth suit, I saw into my beautiful soul, I believe for the first time in my entire life . . . the truth that we are spiritual beings having a physical experience resonated to the very core of my being. It wasn't until my earth suit got out of the way that I was able to finally see me, love me, and connect with me . . . beautiful, courageous me peering out of that earth suit! This is one of my most beautiful discoveries yet! I will never look at myself the same again.

My hair started growing back about two weeks ago! My youngest daughter asked me, "How long will you have fuzz on your head and when will your hair 'really' grow back?"

I said to her, "Let's celebrate. This is a sign of new life for me . . . I even shampooed it for fun!" Even though it is just a shadow of hair covering my head . . . it is a sign of healing and new growth!

I have had seven weeks off since my last chemo, and I know I'm in for twelve more rounds so there is a chance I'll lose it again . . . but for today, I have new hair and that is a sign of hope for me! I know if I lose it again, it does grow back. Lord, if you will it, I would love it if I could keep my hair during the next rounds of chemo . . .

Jesus: Know that my will is for your ultimate freedom from everything that burdens your soul and holds you back from knowing how beautiful you are to me with or without hair. Do not fear, my little one, I will use everything that comes your way for an ultimate good within you that will far outweigh any momentary inconveniences that you experience through this trial. Trust in the plans I have for you . . . they are infinite. "What is seen is temporary . . . what is unseen is eternal" (2 Corinthians 4:18).

May 18, 2006

"Then they cried out to the Lord in their trouble, and he brought them out of their distress. He stilled the storm to a whisper; the waves of the sea were hushed. They were glad when it grew calm, and he guided them to their desired haven" (Psalm 107:28–31).

"And the God of all grace, who called you to his eternal glory in Christ, after you have suffered a little while, will himself restore you and make you strong, firm and steadfast" (1 Peter 5:10).

Me: My pathology report did not come back the way I wanted it to! The cancer was in seven out of the twelve lymph nodes that they removed during the double mastectomy. This means I will need chest wall radiation . . . possibly every day for five weeks on top of twelve more weeks of chemo! I wanted to avoid that because of reconstruction and yet after crying and praying about it, I feel God is calling me to an even deeper sense of surrender and detachment from my flesh . . . establishing even more profoundly the truth that my beauty flows from my soul out. I am choosing to trust that you have a greater good for me . . . that there is more for me to learn in order to grow in love which always leads to more freedom within my soul as a result of going through more of this storm . . . help me to trust in that truth! Right now, I am angry!

Lord, you have given to me a physical sign of perseverance under trial. My heart shaped wreath on my front door has a little bird's nest in it with six small eggs. This bird chose this spot to bring in new life in spite of all the opposition it faced. The door is continually being open and shut throughout the day. Our cat will occasionally jump up on the screen . . . hanging from his front claws as he peers into the nest through the screen door. This bird continues to guard its nest. It continues to fight for the life it is trying to bring into the world. To me, Lord, this is a nest of life and hope sent by you to encourage my soul to fight the fight and run the race with hope in my heart. This cancer continues to knock me down, and your power within me refuses to let me stay down. I wept with my dad when I got my pathology report back after surgery. I cried out to you, "I just want a break . . . just one break in all of this!"

That moment with my dad was one of the closest moments of my life, and I will store that within my heart forever. It was the first time I witnessed my dad weeping. I held him and he cried out, "Enough! I can't take seeing my daughter suffer like this!" we wept in each other's arms. He held me . . . bald and breastless . . . he witnessed to me the love I believe you have for me, Jesus, and I believe you weep with me through this as you did with Mary over the death of Lazarus. How all of this is going to work together for an ultimate good . . . I cannot see yet. I was at a low point once again. As I looked in the mirror at myself the other day, I raised my hands to you after surveying the physical damage this cancer has brought upon my body . . . steri-strips where my breasts used to be . . . and now a large lump under my clavicle, the port they inserted for chemo and its extra-large because they didn't have a petite one during surgery. I am speechless recalling this image of a body that I don't recognize . . . an androgynous figure standing before me . . . bald and breastless . . . I used to be told that I resemble Julia Roberts, now I look like something from another planet. The timing of all this sucks! I wish I had a husband to validate me as a woman . . . I know I am still a woman in here! Lord, I trust in your promises, and I am trusting that you will restore to me tenfold what has been taken from me through this experience and through my grief and sadness . . . emotionally, physically, and spiritually, I trust that you will restore. As the Scripture says, you call me by name, you know I am suffering and you promise to restore me, strengthen me and make me feel firm and steadfast in my soul and life.

Bring it on, Lord! Rain it down . . . fill me up and once again set my feet on solid ground! May your glory be revealed through my life and through this trial . . . may souls be encouraged knowing that you are faithful to your promises. You bring it and I will proclaim it. Yesterday, life burst forth within the nest . . . several little pink birds entered the world in spite of the dangers that surrounded them. Burst forth your life within my soul today Lord . . . in spite of all that surrounds me . . . bring forth the abundant life you promise.

I can't get beyond my image in the mirror. It haunts me . . . I know you love me from my heart out . . . I fear that no one else will be able to look beyond these scars and see my true beauty . . . if I can't how can I expect man to?

Jesus: I am . . . I am the God of all comfort . . . the same comfort that continually flows through my heart I send into yours. Do not fear, my child, do not be afraid . . . what should it matter if the whole world should come against you when your heart is at peace within? Once again . . . victory is yours . . . the battle has been won! It is finished . . . rise up and grab hold of the blessings that I am sending your way . . . pray for eyes to see . . . ears to hear all that I have in store for you! The words of man come to nothing when up against the truths of God. Let my truth be your anchor in the midst of this storm . . . know me, Lauren . . . even if all twelve lymph nodes where infected, what does it matter when you are filled with the same power that rose your Christ from the dead? That is your victory.

Remember who you are and the one who fights your battles. Is anything too hard for me when I have overcome death itself? That is why I say to you . . . do not fear, little one . . . do not look at the waves that surround you, look into my eyes and prepare yourself for abundant restoration! Avoid the image you see in the mirror . . . look at yourself as you are reflected through the eyes of those who authentically see you and love you. Mirrors will always rob you of the truth and mask the essence and source of your true beauty. Remember your mother's insight . . . some cultures do not have mirrors, relying on their inner self-awareness; they reflect their true identity from their soul out into the world. Man looks at the outer appearance . . . God looks at the heart.

Me: Lord, I abandon myself to you. You are my way, my truth, and my life. Be the gatekeeper of my heart, mind and soul . . . allow your perfect love to drive out all fear . . . love is all I desire. Help me to see myself through the eyes of love.

May 24, 2006

"If you make the Most High your dwelling—even the Lord, who is my refuge—For he will command his angels concerning you to guard you in all your ways; they will lift you up in their hands, so that you will not strike your foot against a stone" (Psalm 91:11-12).

Me: Lord, I was knocked down today after talking to my oncologist . . . I questioned the amount of lymph nodes that I had infected and mentioned the fact that no one that I have spoken to so far has had that many infected . . . so what does that mean for me? He said that there are four groups and I fall in the third to highest group for recurrence. Before Herceptin and this second chemo, the chances of this coming back would be 50/50 for me. However, because of the new drugs my odds are much better. I got off the phone and wept . . . once again, I could feel the relentless presence of fear overwhelming my soul. I have stage three cancer. Help me, Lord, not to live in fear . . . the thought of having to go through this again is more than I can handle! I am at a place of surrender to you. I have nowhere else to go to be set free from this fear that paralyzes my whole being! Renew me once again . . . I want this to be finished.

Jesus: Here the words, my child, from my love letter to you . . . Affliction shall not rise up a second time! I send my words to you to heal you of your affliction . . . more than the physical . . . to the depths of your soul . . . to set you free from the chains of fear that hold you back from embracing the fullness of love and courage that already fill your soul. Rise up and cast off the veil of deceit that continually whispers lies to you in your weakened state . . . turn your eyes away from the affliction and fix your vision upon me and my promises to you! My power is completely present to heal you and bind up your wounds and broken heart. You have everything you need to win this battle. I tell you and encourage you to believe so completely in the deliverance and victory that I offer you, that you dance and sing your way with full confidence, that victory is yours, and that this affliction will not rise up a second time. Nothing is impossible with God.

Me: Only speak one word, and I shall be healed and set free from all fear. I desire to have such confidence in your ability to heal and save me that I will dance and sing through this trial, proclaiming your love and faithfulness along the way, I believe that this is possible with you in me . . . yet help my unbelief in my weakened state. I'm having a hard time right now.

May 28, 2006

"If I speak in the tongues of men and of angels, but have not love, I am only a resounding gong or a clanging cymbal. If I have the gift of prophecy and can fathom all mysteries and all knowledge, and if I have a faith that can move mountains, but have not love, I am nothing. If I give all I possess to the poor and surrender my body to the flames, but have not love, I gain nothing" (1 Corinthians 13:1–3).

Me: Lord, I feel as if you are unveiling a part of life that has always surrounded me, yet I walked in its presence unaware of the true beauty it possessed. In this new vision that you have graced me with, through this cancer, there is no fear . . . as I lay still and ponder the reality of this truth, I am experiencing within my soul this tremendous sense of courage and anticipation for my life with you at the center of it.

I'm amazed at how many fears held me captive before this trial Fear to be true to my heart for fear of judgments. Fear of failure in life. Fear of being alone. Fear of rejection. Fear of being vulnerable. Fear of loving without being loved back. Fear of letting go of everything and trusting you to lead me into my desired haven. Fear of fear itself. Your message of love has set me free again and again of all fear. I trust that you will continue to set me free no matter what may come my way.

Jesus: I say to you, Lauren, fear not! This is the essence of my message. There is no room for fear in the presence of perfect love. All souls that choose to live their life in me and aware of my infinite love for them are empowered with the ability to love freely without fear . . . and to open themselves up to being loved without fear. Every negative emotion that pulls your soul away from true joy has its foundation built on fear. Truly, truly I say to you, true love embodies trust, selflessness, hope, perseverance, and courage. All of these traits take root, grow and ultimately fill the soul with life and light in the absence of fear.

Approach any fear or result of fear head on . . . glance at it briefly then quickly turn to the infinite love that continuously flows from my heart into yours and allow it to burn up all fear based thoughts and intentions. Be free, my beautiful child . . . in all you do be free . . . love deeply, laugh freely and live passionately. Without love you have nothing and you gain nothing . . . with love you have everything and gain everything you need for this life and the life to come.

June 6, 2006

"We love because he first loved us" (1 John 4:19).

"God is love. Whoever lives in love lives in God, and God in him" (1 John 4:16).

Me: Lord, speak to me . . . tell me your words of love and inspiration. I start chemo again on Wednesday . . . twelve straight weeks of chemo followed by six weeks of daily radiation, and then I will finish up with reconstruction sometime next year. This is the end of the race Lord . . . the last mountain to climb in my journey through my cancer experience. You have surrounded me with beautiful people . . . souls that you put on my heart to love and encourage in this life are now being used by you to love and encourage my soul. I am rendered speechless, and I am filled with an overwhelming sense of gratitude for this gift . . . I want this love to reach every cell in my body and replace anything that is bent on destruction or fear within me so that when I emerge from this battle and the dust around me is cleared away I will be complete and fully aware that it is love that saved me. I will walk with confidence in each step . . . my head held high, my shoulders back . . . I will walk forward into my new life transformed by love . . . empowered by your amazing grace to go forth and love, maybe for the first time, freely, uninhibited, unencumbered, unlimited, and deeply committed to my calling to love others, as you have taught me so intimately through this trial, as I love myself. I love because I have been loved by you in so many beautiful ways through this storm.

Jesus: You are my beautiful little flower of love to the world with the heart of a lion! Rise up once again, my child; rise and walk with confidence knowing that the one you have entrusted with your battle and victory will bring it to pass. Remember the one who has faith has the strength and ability within to cast down mountains and throw them into the sea. You have the courage of a lion, my little warrior for life; prepare yourself once again for battle with confidence knowing it is already won. Rise up and walk to victory. I am the Lion of Judah . . . my strength will carry you through the moments of pain and weakness that you fear . . . my heart beats through yours.

Contemplate the courage of the lion. Is there anything in all of creation that he truly fears? You continue to rise up and walk forward because you are empowered by perfect love . . . a love that drives out all fear. A true warrior fights from a heart full of passion . . . love fuels passion. You are a passionate warrior for love in this world. Your journey has only just begun. Your eyes have not seen; your ears have not heard; your mind cannot conceive the fullness of life that God has prepared for you. Surrendering to love is your strength, my beautiful one, with eager expectation for what God will give to you as each new day of life unfolds before your eyes.

June 9, 2006

"Never will I leave you; never will I forsake you" (Hebrews 13:5).

Me: Lord . . . I have been given a gift from you today . . . even if it is only one day, I rejoice in how great I feel after today's chemo treatment. I have absolutely no symptoms. I am so thankful for a break in all of this. I can develop bone pain up to forty-eight to seventy-two hours after my treatment. I commit those hours to you God . . . you promise never to leave my side. Even if the pain should start tomorrow, the joy and strength I feel today will carry me through it . . . thank you for this moment of relief.

Jesus: In all things give thanks, little warrior. Your faith has carried you through this day . . . trust and faith . . . with these two qualities at your side there is never a battle that you will face that will not cease to end in total victory! You will not shrink back and be destroyed by the storms of life. You have the same power within you that conquered death and rose my defeated flesh from the grave . . . proving the truth that nothing can harm your soul when it is connected to its creator. Even if the flesh is destroyed, when the eyes of your soul are linked in a convicted gaze of love with mine, you will always walk on top of the tumultuous waters of life!

Me: I love you, Jesus. Protect your little flower. You have given me the heart of a lion. I am beginning to realize that and celebrate it!

June 20, 2006

"And know these three remain: faith, hope and love. But the greatest of these is love" (1 Corinthians 13:13).

Me: I am giving myself over to a sweet surrender to the moments in my life . . . I breathe deeper, laugh deeper, give deeper, and love God, myself, and others more honestly, freely, and completely. I've never experienced this deep sense of awareness to the fact that I am free to dance and sing when I am moved to do so . . . without boundaries. Through it all I'm finding myself caught up in this beautiful free-flowing continual dance of love within the depths of my soul . . . I am loved, I am whole, and I am complete. I do not need anyone or anything to validate this truth. God has said . . . let it be so and that is enough for me. You love me, God . . . all of me and because of that no one and no thing can take this truth away from me. Yet, I am choosing to invite people and experiences into this dance of life and love I am experiencing . . . to expand my world, deepen my character, challenge my faith, and share your omnipotent, omnipresent, unshakable, unlimited, unconditional, inspirational, passionate, creative love with me. This is the kind of dance that will lead my soul into eternity . . . one that I refuse to sit out on as I watch others dance by . . . no more spectating for me . . . I have entered the dance of life. At times, my feet grow weary, my body aches, and my steps are sluggish yet the beat of your love, poured into me courses through the veins of my very being and the source of its power, strengthens my weak knees and feeble hands. Once again, I rise up renewed. My soul dances with beauty and ease as I feel the same power that raised your wounded body from the grave, pulsate through my body and soul. With every breath I take I am once again restored, renewed, and strengthened . . . all because you are in me; I am in you and we are one. I am truly captivated these days by your love. I feel intoxicated by the beauty of your presence within me. Yes, I am waking up from my slumber . . . I am waking up to a new sense of self and life!

You never fail to touch me with detail in my life. My dad gave me a gift of beautiful flower gardens on my property to celebrate my life. I decided to pick all of the flowers that captivated me throughout my life. In fact, I am calling it the Garden of Life. I forgot to tell the landscaper that I wanted a rose bush. Roses, as you know, Lord, are some of my favorite flowers. I love how you mixed thorns in with tremendously intoxicating beauty and fragrance. In fact, when I smell and see roses, I completely overlook all of the thorns. They remind me of my life. Sometimes all I feel and see are thorns, yet as I grow older, I also grow in confidence throughout the thorny moments knowing that the rose is on its way. When it comes, the thorns will be quickly overlooked, as the beauty of the rose captivates my eye. You sent me a beautiful rose bush yesterday, knowing how it would fill my heart with joy so great that it overflowed through my eyes! The landscaper said when he saw it; he was moved to get it for me even though I didn't ask for it. He told me it will produce some of the most beautiful roses I will ever see. I am once again rendered silent . . . in awe of all you do to continually win my heart to yours!

I just had another chemo today. It took five hours again . . . yet I feel untouched because my soul is so full of your love and the love of those around me now more than ever. True love for myself. I have so much to give out, Lord, and

I am excited about this dance of love called life before me. Hold me close, Jesus . . . let me always hear the beat of your heart. Grant me the confidence and grace to let go and trust knowing you already know all of the steps I need to take in order to enter into the fullness of life and love . . . lead me on, oh, beautiful Lord of my dance!

Jesus: Beautiful rose of my eternal garden. Your love captivates my heart. I continually long for a glance, a pause in your day where you look into me within you . . . a lifting of your heart and voice to my throne of love . . . you are so easily pleased by all of the love notes that I leave you throughout your day. My heart is held captive to every thought, every expression of gratitude that you direct my way. I am everywhere for you, Lauren . . . everything that surrounds your day has the potential of drawing you closer to me and to you. I delight in every word of love, gratitude, and simple thoughts and desires that you offer to me throughout your day. I love you, Lauren . . . it is not stagnant, nor is it based on conditions. This kind of love moves with every breath you take, every thought you think, every move you make during your life on earth. Continue to seek love above all things. Truly, I say to you, you will receive all of the passion and love you desire and it will carry you into eternity. The kind of love that I offer you will never cease to leave you with a full sense of freedom and wholeness . . . lacking nothing. Yes, it is as you say . . . trust and continue to love with my love, knowing it is unlimited. And as it will be with your beautiful gardens, it will grow more beautiful with time! More fragrance, more color, more blooms, and, yes, more thorns, yet the beauty, fragrance, and all of the life your garden will draw unto itself (birds, bees, and butterflies) will far outweigh any potential weeds and thorns. Always focus on the beauty of life. Where your treasure is, your heart will follow.

One more thought for you, my little rose . . . think about the love and joy in your dad's voice when he heard how the gardens he gave to you moved you to tears of joy. How much greater my joy is when I see that my creations stir your soul so deeply. I made these for you and I rejoice over the truth that they have captivated your heart . . . that my love for you, in you and around you moves you to tears of joy. I tell you, this makes my joy complete! Know that you are always surrounded in the garden of my love.

July 10, 2006

"Find rest, O my soul, in God alone; my hope comes from him. He alone is my rock and my salvation; he is my fortress, I will not be shaken. My salvation and my honor depend on God; he is my mighty rock, my refuge. Trust in him at all times O people; pour out your hearts to him for God is our refuge" (Psalm 62:5–8).

Me: Lord, I have seven more chemos to go. Last week, I was accidentally given a double dose of the steroid that I need to take with the chemo to cut down on bone pain. I was up all night . . . I knew something was not right; I had a hard time catching my breath, and I felt like my heart was going to pound out of my chest. I know that one of the side effects to the medicine I am taking is heart damage, and I am choosing to turn that over to you. Lord, every heartbeat is in the palm of your hand. Thank you for sustaining my life throughout the nights and days. I am grateful these days for every heartbeat . . . every breath. Help me once again to see every circumstance that comes my way during this trial as an opportunity for learning, surrendering, and growth. My life is all about love and trust.

Jesus: You have a physical heartbeat and an eternal heartbeat . . . that remains untouched by any earthly trauma. Focus on the eternal heartbeat . . . it will never cease to pump the essence of true life throughout your soul!

JULY 11, 2006

"Consider it pure joy, my brothers, whenever you face trials of many kinds, because you know that the testing of your faith develops perseverance. Perseverance must finish its work so that you may be mature and complete, not lacking anything. If any of you lacks wisdom, he should ask God, who gives generously to all without finding fault, and it will be given to him" (James 1:2–4).

Me: Lord, I haven't written about my divorce yet . . . even though it has been taking place at the same time as my cancer experience. I am ready now. Thank you for the gift of my children. They continually fill my heart with joy and hope. Seventeen years is a long time. I married at 21, and I can't remember a lot of my thinking at that time except to say that I loved you then. This last year you have healed a lot of wounds left on my heart . . . feelings of anger, hurt, rejection, and confusion have been slowly replaced with forgiveness, strength, acceptance, and understanding. Many people have asked me how I am dealing with two of the top stressors in life (cancer and divorce) at the same time and still be able to love and laugh. My answer: moment by moment . . . letting go of all I see and trusting in your vision, your insights, your purpose for me, and ultimately your love for me. You have promised to restore, establish, set free, renew, strengthen, and comfort all souls who are open to your presence within. I will testify to the truth that you have never forsaken me or abandoned me even during the darkest nights of my soul! The darker the night, the brighter the light of your love became within my heart. You have seen my broken heart; you have witnessed the depth of my despair throughout countless nights that I have cried out to you for help. Not once . . . *not once* have you failed to reveal your presence to me in the midst of my pain.

You are teaching me how to embrace being real and honest about the woman I am. I am reclaiming all of the pieces of me that I lost over time and discovering who I truly am and seeing all that you are calling me to be. This is a wonderful journey to full life! Am I grieving? *Yes*! I am grieving the loss of a dream . . . A dream that I clung to for seventeen years. Many times, I honored the sacred vow over my own heart.

Jesus: St. John experienced a profound depth of insight and revelation within his soul as a result of experiencing the trial of ultimate rejection during his exile to the Island of Patmos. Bring all of your feelings, fears, and pain into the Holy of Holies and you will always walk out with deep revelations from the heavenly realms that will transform your soul and vision forever. Every trial becomes a tool in the hand of the master artist to refine and set free the human heart. Too often, you do not give this job over. John gave himself over to me completely during his exile. I then was able to give myself completely over to him. He then recorded the many great revelations that took place during our intimate moments together. Surrender is the door that you must pass through in order to experience life-changing intimacy with your God. You will then have ears to hear, eyes to see, and the strength to overcome all trials and tribulations that you will face in this world and in the spiritual realms.

Your Heavenly Father created man and woman, yet he does not bring every man and woman together. There is free choice . . . you can choose. Know that God will always bring good out of every choice you make when you choose him through it. Commit all your ways to Him and then surrender, knowing that I will lead you to where your plans will succeed. Trials are a part of walking through your journey on earth. My greatest gift to you is not to spare you of these trials. Suffering, when surrendered, produces beautiful character and results in profound wisdom, understanding and freedom.

My gift to you is not to save you from earthly trials but to bring about a greater good within you than there was before the trial began. I create, with my Father, beauty and love within the soul. The good within our hearts is so immense that it ultimately swallows up the pain of any trial experienced on earth . . . so much so that the human heart will even experience a depth of gratitude for the trial because of the fortitude, character, and strength that it has gained walking through the fire. Truly, I say unto you it is the refiner's fire that perfects the silver and gold . . . it is the trial at hand that becomes the refining tool that ultimately enables the soul to consider itself fortunate in the midst of suffering. The end result will always outweigh any pain endured through the storms of life when your eyes are fixed on the eternal experience, self-awareness, and love.

The world will question your strength and peace when you show it under trial. The world does not comprehend the eternal . . . for many it is foolishness, yet under trial, every soul searches for meaning and purpose. How the trial is received makes all the difference between overcoming and being overcome. You have free choice just as Peter did . . . will you focus on the storms and waves of life or will you keep your eyes fixed on the one who has taught you how to walk on top of water?

Me: No more unmet expectations. I choose you once again. My only way, my one truth, and my fullest life. Truly, you are my divine physician . . . the one most skilled to heal my broken heart and mend my crushed spirit. Truly, you are my bodyguard.

August 28, 2006

"See how the lilies of the field grow. They do not labor or spin" (Matthew 11:28).

Me: Lord, the rose bush that you brought into my life in the beginning of this summer is producing the most beautiful roses I have ever seen!

Jesus: Consider the state of the rose . . . in the midst of the thorns the most captivating beauty emerges. So too with suffering . . . out of suffering emerges authentic beauty that is beyond compare as well as radiance and depth of character that reflects true wisdom and peace.

SEPTEMBER 13, 2006

"Not that I have already obtained all this, or have already been made perfect, but I press on to take hold of that for which Christ Jesus took hold of me. Brothers, I do not consider myself yet to have taken hold of it. But one thing I do: Forgetting what is behind and straining toward what is ahead, I press on toward the goal to win the prize for which God has called me heavenward in Christ Jesus" (Philippians 3:12–14).

Me: Today, I started radiation for six straight weeks every day . . . truly the last leg of this cancer race in my mind . . . funny, I keep saying that. I will have my second reconstruction surgery on December 6th. Mentally, for me, the biggest hurdles will be behind me . . . what is left is just clean up after the battle. As I reflect on 9/11, I have this image of myself walking out of the smoke after surviving the collapse of the buildings. Yes, I am a survivor. I have survived a life-threatening disease that set-up camp in my body . . . I won. No cell that is bent on destruction has a place in this body of mine. I reflect life and light not death and darkness!

A friend of mine, who is also a survivor, said she felt that no one would love her war-torn body after cancer. I can relate to this fear. As I reflected on this, some very strong emotions welled up within me. Our bodies have protected us, and we have won the battle. We have battle scars that reflect strength, courage, and most importantly victory! Along with these scars we have emerged from the rubble with a new sense of freedom and a new-found awareness of the beautiful women we are . . . this beauty is not based on hair, breasts, or anything physical but on the true essence of who we are in relation to the one who created us. We see ourselves as God sees us . . . from the heart out. Our self-esteem is steadfast in the knowledge that no one or no thing (disease or circumstance) can touch our true identity that rests within our soul . . . this is true freedom. We have been stripped down emotionally and physically as we have fought this battle for life, yet our souls have remained untouched. From our souls flow the truth of who we are and contain the potential of all we are called to be. What a beautiful experience to know the reality of that truth and now we have the opportunity to live this life victoriously in the freedom that comes from loving ourselves as God loves us.

I believe that we will attract other souls who share the same understanding of life. Those souls that are still blinded by the allure of the things that bind and control us in this world will simply pass through our lives leaving us untouched because we know who we are. This kind of self-regard allows us to view others right where they are without judging them because we know that they cannot threaten or damage the essence of our identity. This leaves us in a beautiful spot to love without attachment. I can now love you, without having to change you to be more like me. I can now love you without feeling threatened that you won't love me back. I can love you simply because I know I am loved from my soul out. I am not needy in my love because I already have all I need. Since I have been stripped of everything through this battle, physically speaking, and I have experienced my soul remaining intact and even strengthened in endless ways through this experience, I know that nothing can take away my true beauty and identity. Our beauty flows from a source that is the same yesterday, today and tomorrow. What should it matter who validates that when we know it to be true? Thank you, Jesus, for instructing my heart in the ways of love through this trial.

Jesus: Knowing and loving who you truly are in light of the trials you are walking through is the essence of the truth that God works all things together for an ultimate good.

OCTOBER 9, 2006

"The Lord does not look at the things man looks at, Man looks at the outward appearance, but the Lord looks at the heart" (1 Samuel 16:7).

Me: I had to deflate one of my breasts that was already inflated through reconstruction in order to get a good angle for radiation. It took about two months of weekly injections to fill up these expanders in my body. I am left with one partial breast and one shriveled up flat breast along with two round scars where my nipples used to be. Lord, I am impatient with the re-growth of my hair and the reconstruction of my body. I only have two and a half more weeks of radiation and for that I cannot express the depth of my joy and gratitude, yet I find myself struggling with the discontent of my heart over the loss of so much of my physical beauty through this . . . it is where I am at today.

Jesus: Never run from where you find yourself emotionally within your heart. Honor those feelings as your body has honored your soul through this trial. Allow yourself to feel the emotions of grief over the change in your physical appearance for a time. I then encourage you to go deeper . . . seek out deeper wisdom and understanding concerning your own beauty through this . . . rebuild your identity on the things that cannot be taken by physical illness in this world. Truly, I say to you, your true identity has remained untouched through this cancer, as has the source of your true beauty. My desire for you in all of your struggles with your physical appearance is that you are able to so deeply root your self-esteem in the beauty that flows from your soul out into the world that any physical sign of outer beauty is looked upon by you as an extension of your inner beauty. Seek that perspective of beauty, and you shall free yourself of much of the inner turmoil that continues to hold you in bondage to the things of the world . . . remember the world and its perspective of beauty passes away but the beauty that radiates from the soul is eternal! Gain wisdom into all of this by allowing your mind and heart to see beyond the physical when you look in the mirror. Remember it is man that looks at his outer appearance, not God . . . God looks at the heart.

From the heart flows the beauty that radiates from the very existence of nature that surrounds you. Nature is guided by the wisdom of eternal beauty. The kind of wisdom that allows the hand of God to gently unfold its beauty rather than forcing open that which is meant to gently unfold with vigilant patience over time, revealing a beauty that is timeless. Contemplate the rose and the butterfly . . . their beauty is born from the wisdom of patience and surrender to God's perfect timing and plan. Commit your eyes to me; ask me to help you see yourself as I do . . . from your beautiful soul out. Anchor your self-image in those things that are unseen . . . gentleness, kindness, patience, humility, love, humor, peace, goodness. I ask you, can any of these be taken away by physical turmoil and trial? From your soul flows the essence of your true identity and your true freedom . . . look within!

October 24, 2006

"Jesus said, 'It is finished" (John 19:30).

Me: My last radiation was today. What am I feeling? Besides getting used to third degree burns all over my chest and getting over the nausea that I feel when I change my bandages twice a day revealing my ripped, burned, bloody skin . . . I feel an overwhelming sense of gratitude to God for my family, my friends, and myself. I feel deep gratitude for all of the strength that flowed from different sources into my broken heart. I have won! Every procedure, every cell bent on destruction and every fear that tried to hold me captive have all been overcome by love. I feel overwhelmingly convicted, now more than ever, that all things are possible with love . . . God is love, and God has loved me through others and has given to me through others everything that I have needed for victory through this battle.

Through my tears and heartache, God has produced within my soul a freedom and confidence that now guides my soul throughout the moments of my day. The freedom to be me without any attachments to the trivial worries that used to bind me to the world. I am free! I have a love for myself that is not based on someone else loving me . . . this type of love breeds many insecurities within the human heart . . . this new-found love is grounded in a deep awareness that true love flows between my heart and God . . . it is in this state of inner awareness that I am experiencing loving others without the need to judge, control or possess them. Rather I can now appreciate and love them for who they are and where they are at from a heart that does not need love and approval in return to know that I am loved and beautiful. Therefore, I can love freely. It is an entirely different experience for me walking through this journey of life. I see . . . I hear . . . I sense . . . I experience everything with a renewed awareness of life through this body of mine . . . this body that has emerged from battle, bruised and broken in many ways yet completely whole within.

Lord, I choose today to be like a child . . . to experience the authenticity, innocence, and freedom that accompany the act of simply being me. I am not my physical appearance; I am my soul expressing myself through my physical experience. My purpose has been made very clear to me through this experience . . . I am here to learn how to love . . . God, others, and myself. Love remains after everything else fades away . . . it is the same yesterday, today, and tomorrow . . . eternally . . . this is love . . . this is life . . . this is you, Jesus . . . this is God.

JANUARY 30, 2007

"He stilled the storm to a whisper; the waves of the sea were hushed. They were glad when it grew calm, and he guided them to their desired haven. Let them give thanks to the Lord for his unfailing love and his wonderful deeds for men" (Psalm 107:29–3).

Me: I have been given the gift of new life. With each new dawn, I have the opportunity to learn how to love better! Even with the physical setbacks with this reconstruction of my body, I have a profound sense of who I am. It seems that every week I had some kind of procedure done. I have learned that as my suffering has increased, love has increased all the more around me and within me to the point that the suffering is swallowed up by love. As I am approaching my one year anniversary from my diagnosis, I am filled with a deep sense of admiration and respect for the strength of character that dwells within this body of mine. When I experience pain and anguish, I am learning how to be gentle with myself. The holidays triggered me back into the grief I shelved over the loss of my marriage. I remember as soon as I was faced with cancer, the emotions around my divorce were shelved in order to save my life. I'm now healthy enough to enter back into the healing process and move on with new life.

I'm going to be under treatment for a while . . . I just went in this week to get some stitches out and was back in two days later for another surgery. I keep seeking a date when all of the treatments and surgeries will be completed . . . no dates in sight. In light of this, I have made the choice not to miss out on life in between. My life takes place in the present moment . . . knowing that my moments will eventually carry me to my desired haven. So here I sit in my chair, writing down my thoughts, breathing in and out . . . I am alive now more than ever before . . . I am alive! I have woken up to your transcendent presence within my entire being. How did I make it to this place of peace after such gut wrenching pain, fear, and anguish? By putting one foot in front of the other, letting life come to me bit by bit, holding the hands that were sent to hold me up, taking one breath at a time, focusing on one moment and then another, and above all looking deep within and resurrecting with God's strength the truth of who I am and knowing the power of divine love and its ability to overcome everything that I feel overcome by. Who am I to worry? Can this add a single hour to my life? The less I cling to this life, the freer I become in my ability to relish, taste, and embrace the moment. Love is perfected in the awareness of the present moment and everything that is exploding in that moment around me . . . the essence of who I am in relation to life, to others, and to God is found in the present moment. Thank you for this conscious awareness to what *is* around me.

Jesus: Remember love is always present . . . your emotions are not meant to be defined, they are meant to be experienced without judgment for they reflect the truth in your heart. Do not try to contain, resist, or control them. Contemplate the river. It simply flows over the rocks effortlessly; allow your emotions to flow without trying to control them. Your greatest pain often comes from your resistance to what is . . . practice the art of allowing and feeling safe in that experience.

June 1, 2007

"Now we see but a poor reflection; then we shall see face to face. Now I know in part; then I shall know fully, even as I am fully known. And now these three remain: faith, hope and love. But the greatest of these is love" (1 Corinthians 13:12–13).

Me: My girlfriend, Susan, has been by my side battling stage four stomach cancer for about eight months now. She is around my age and has a husband and two beautiful children. She is a warrior in the deepest sense of the word. She has modeled to me what it means to accept what is and how to walk through the fire with dignity, courage, humility, and love. She has been a soul sister to me in countless ways. She is the kind of person that looks into my soul with unwavering eye contact that resonates with unspoken wisdom and understanding. She has a smile that brightens up a room and the hearts of those who encounter it . . . she has never ceased to smile through all of this . . . in spite of the fact that she has endured countless setbacks and intense pain. She has been on a feeding tube since December, and her positive attitude is beyond what I have ever encountered . . . she is a city set on a hill, and she shines through all of this pain.

Today, I am silenced by the presence of divine wisdom that is pouring out effortlessly through the beautiful mouth of my beloved friend. Here she is forty-eight hours before entering into the heavenly realms . . . with such a profound resolve and acceptance of death, I am rendered silent. As I lay in this hospital bed next to my friend, who has become my spiritual mentor, I soak in every word . . . listening to her say goodbye for now to all of her family and friends with such confidence, dignity, and resolve. Susan tearfully speaks the words from the mouth of an angel. I am writing as fast as I can, knowing that these words are pieces of gold sent from the heart of eternal love himself . . . jewels of wisdom that I believe come to us when we stand on the threshold of heaven and earth. In the words of my beloved friend Susan, who now dances with the angels in heaven:

"The most important lessons in life: find peace in your heart and live by your heart. If you live by your heart and through your heart, you are living by Jesus. Jesus gives me peace . . . Jesus has helped me through this monstrosity, and he is going to take care of me, and he is going to tell me when it's time to go. It may not always be the way you want it in the end . . . but, on the other hand, you know and have the comfort of knowing that he is the ultimate peace . . . we can wait and wait and wait to try to get peace, and we'll know that he will ultimately bring us peace . . . it's not our way . . . it's not our thinking. Jesus is my rock, and it is all about him right now . . . it has always been about him and his love . . . it is not my way . . . it is not my thinking . . . it is his way and his thinking now . . . and through him I will find ultimate happiness. At this point, it's not about putting my family or myself or my friends first . . . it's about what I believe is Jesus' will for me. Through his will I get the peace that passes all human understanding. In the midst of pain and emotional hurt, Jesus revealed to my heart that when people act out their pain . . . he said that they just haven't been loved enough. It all comes down to love. People are unkind because of fear and lack of love . . . it all comes down to love." —Susan Maier October 20, 1964–June 3, 2007

So true my beautiful friend . . . it all comes down to love in the end . . . love given, received, and withheld. Susan and

I held each other and wept. "I'm going to miss your physical presence so much Susan."

Susan, speaking through her tears says, "Lauren, we will always be together . . . we just have to figure out how to do this long-distance relationship for a while. Look for me, Lauren, I'm going to come to you through robins . . . I know they fill your heart with hope. So, expect me to come to you through them."

Susan died less than forty-eight hours after sharing those words with me.

Jesus: To you it's death and grieving . . . to the heavens, it is life and the celebration of a beautiful homecoming! Remember, sometimes the righteous are taken home young to spare them from worldly turmoil and trials. Every tear is wiped away in the full presence of divine love. Eternal wisdom gives peace to all that you question on earth. In an instant, everything that is unknown is known. Everything that is unseen is seen. Everything that is misunderstood is understood. Everything that has been twisted because of pain and fear is made whole and complete through the refining fire of divine love . . . in an instant, my child. Remember exhale once on earth, inhale your next breath in heaven . . . there is simply a thin veil that separates the two.

June 5, 2006

"Therefore, since we are surrounded by such a great cloud of witnesses, let us throw off everything that hinders and the sin that so easily entangles, and let us run with perseverance the race marked out for us" (Hebrews 12:1).

Me: As I was driving today, I began to weep because I missed Susan . . . so much so that my body ached. I pulled my car over on the side of the road because I couldn't see the road through the waterfall of tears. As I was pulling off a huge robin swooped by my windshield, then another and another and another . . . I counted seven robins . . . which also happens to be my favorite number! Without a doubt, Susan had figured out how to work the robin thing to reach me from heaven. When I got home, two robins were sitting side by side in my driveway, and they would not move . . . I got out and walked up to them, just a foot away . . . they didn't budge . . . so I stood, gazing upon these two beautiful birds in a silent meditative state. I stood embracing the moment and opening myself up to Susan's words, "I will come to you, Lauren, through robins." whenever I hear a robin sing, I know it's Susan, borrowing this little bird's melodic song to send me a message of love and hope from heaven.

Jesus: Never underestimate the power of love . . . its creativity and detail. Remember, Lauren, there is only a thin veil that separate heaven and earth . . . you are constantly surrounded by a great cloud of witnesses who send messages of love and hope. Soon you will see her face to face . . . for now, she uses the robin's song to remind you of the beautiful truths she spoke about on her deathbed. I see it as the bed of true wisdom and life.

June 28, 2007

"The righteous cry out, and the Lord hears them; he delivers them from all their troubles. The Lord is close to the brokenhearted and saves those who are crushed in spirit. A righteous man may have many troubles, but the Lord delivers him from them all" (Psalm 34:17–19).

Me: Well . . . if I'm going to learn to love myself, God, and others better then I need to embrace the art of *letting go*! Today, I'm practicing. They are removing my left implant so that I can heal. Yes, so that I can heal and love myself no matter what I look like and also experience the love of those around me.

In January, I got a staph infection that spread to my blood stream. I was in the hospital for five days. Since then I have been getting infection after infection after infection because of the radiated skin. I have also had numerous surgeries.

I was in a fashion show recently with a woman who had a double mastectomy as well, she showed me her chest, and I have to say it was beautiful . . . she didn't have any radiation and her skin was beautiful. My skin was like a crispy piece of bacon, and in light of that, I think it's looking awesome compared to where it was. I have used EFT (Emotional Freedom Technique) along with drinking tons of aloe vera and the results are amazing. I know that God led me to both of these gifts for healing. I met a woman the other day who said if it were not for her loving husband that she would have a hard time with it all. Wow, it's amazing to me how as women, we long to have that validation and support. It's built into our system, and we all want to be adored, pursued, and loved. To me, that is such a powerful testimony to the fact that we are created in the image of God . . . who desires to be adored, pursued, and loved. I have wondered if I would have let go of the pursuit to get my breasts back if I was married to a man who felt the way about me that this woman's husband does. I have also looked at my situation as a profound opportunity to give myself the validation, love, and support that I long to receive from a man. I am thankful for this experience, and I do not shrink from all of the potential it holds to lead me into an unspoken bliss of simply being me and loving all of me. I forgot who I was, and therefore, I farmed out the power to define me to the world around me. I am realizing that my sense of self-worth is completely an inside job with two positions: God—CEO, Lauren—President . . . that's it. Thank you, God, for another day of life to learn how to love better.

Jesus: Yes, all things in life are an opportunity for learning and growing in the grace of self-awareness, trust, acceptance, peace, patience, joy, kindness, goodness, gentleness, and most importantly . . . love.

June 30, 2007

"But seek first his kingdom and his righteousness, and all these things will be given to you as well. Therefore do not worry about tomorrow, for tomorrow will worry about itself" (Matthew 6:33–34).

Me: Well, the breast has been removed . . . once again. My body is so relieved; I feel as if it's singing the hallelujah choir. I didn't think I would look at me again so soon, but I had to change the bandages, and it's not as bad as I was imagining it to be . . . I'm learning that to be the case more often than not. I have some honkin' battle wounds . . . yet I am gaining so much self-respect through all of this . . . I am thinking . . . just a little bit . . . that this whole experience has been the greatest gift to me in my entire life . . . is that crazy or what?

These wounds represent victory . . . I am still standing on this earth to look at them all. I have won. My body resembles that of a courageous, beautiful warrior . . . I have entered the narrow gate that has resulted in a profound understanding of my purpose in life. The struggle to enter that gate is reflected by these scars on my flesh. As my beautiful girlfriend Susan said, "It all comes down to love!"

Jesus: I make all things work for an ultimate good that far outweighs the trial itself. Embracing this truth will ease your discontent and worries.

January 23, 2008

"For I did not come to judge the world, but to save it" (John 12:47).

"Ask and it will be given to you; seek and you shall find; knock and the door will be opened to you. For everyone who asks receives he who knocks, the door will be opened" (Matthew 7:7–8).

Me: I am about to walk into my eleventh and final reconstructive surgery in less than two years . . . this is what is going through my mind, Lauren, why in the heck did you go through all of these surgeries just to have breasts again? Why couldn't you let them go and be okay with the blank scared chest? Are you that vain? Good questions . . . Lord, remember when I was holding onto the left breast and couldn't give it up even though I had so many infections? Finally, when I had them take it out . . . again, my body rejoiced with relief as I wept at the sight of me. Even though I don't fully know why I have endured eleven surgeries to have breasts, I have learned to accept and love myself right where I am at . . . just as you accept me, God. Maybe this is my biggest lesson . . . Even though I'm not perfect, I deeply and completely love and accept myself anyway. Maybe it is vanity, maybe it's my inability to accept being breastless at forty and single, maybe it's my fear of rejection, maybe it's simply having a hard time surveying the damage day in and day out and all that the damage triggers inside me during my weak moments, maybe it's because, for me, walking into this final surgery represents closure and crossing the finish line or better yet emerging from the storm still intact, maybe I didn't give up wanting to restore completely what the cancer had taken . . . maybe it's not about these breasts at all, maybe it's about complete restoration in my heart and mind for my sense of victory, peace, and well-being. I have friends who decided not to reconstruct for their own reasons and they are beautiful. It's not about comparison anymore for me, it's about my relationship with God and myself in God and with God . . . from this bond, I can freely love and accept all of me, just as I am. Seeing me from a place of loving observation and acceptance rather than from a place of judgment has liberated my soul, enabling me to give the same gift of love and acceptance to every person that flows through my life. Thank you, Jesus, for being such a beautiful example of love when you walked this earth . . . your love was so great it moved the hearts of everyone who encountered you to want to choose love over everything.

Jesus: I have come not to judge but to guide hearts into the mission of love in this world. It begins within your own heart. Continue to know, seek, knock, and ask. Make it your life's ambition to unleash the abundance of love that already dwells within you. For as your friend Susan said before she entered the heavenly realm, "Love is the only thing you get to bring with you . . . in the end, nothing else matters." If you have love, you have everything . . . remember this truth and use it as the foundation for all of your moments. Remember, love is always present. When you remain present and embrace the presence of love in each moment, all of life will radiate with abundance!

June 16, 2008

"I in them and you in me. May they be brought to complete unity to let the world know that you sent me and have loved them even as you have loved me" (John 17:23).

Me: Lord, my understanding of this whole experience has shifted from one of war to one of acceptance and peace. As a result of this surrender and reconnection to *all* parts of me, the greatest strength, healing and sense of well-being has emerged within me. I began this journey from the perspective of war. I was the warrior battling this terrible *disease* in my body. The pain has become for me the portal to peace through which I have been able to see, connect with, and love all that I am. Including the cancer. When I experience any discomfort now I simply talk to my body:

"What is the message behind this pain?"

"What are you trying to tell me body?"

"Do I need to let go of something? Guard my heart? Speak my truth? Set boundaries? Or maybe you are telling me to forgive, accept the situation, accept myself or another person, slow down, remain present, let go of judgment, rest, be patience, trust."

"Or maybe this is a message for me to release all fear, doubt and worry."

All of these messages flow from you in me and all from God. They are opportunities for me to bring love and acceptance into the present situation, the present moment. This experience enables me to be fully present to you in all things.

I have also learned that any physical ailment I encounter has an emotional foundation. Lord, you have made my body so magnificently! My body tries to protect me from uncomfortable feelings and experiences like, anger, abandonment, grief, trauma, fear, resentment, and rejection. Its very creativity is unmatched in its methods of *storing* this pain. Behind all of my physical pain is a repressed emotional pain that has been stored away. This is brilliant, Lord! By identifying the source of my pain and surrendering through the experience of loving and accepting myself completely even though I have the pain, I am able to enter into the experience of feeling safe in my body which then creates the perfect environment within me for healing and restoration.

Lord, every trauma and trial in my life resulted in some form of disconnect between you and me, me and others and ultimately me and myself. My body did the best it could at the time to deal with it, and as a result, over time, I became so disconnected with the true essence of who I truly am as created in your image that I felt unsafe living in this world and in my body. Letting go and coming to peace with my emotional pains from my past and my sense of self that was attached to them has led me into this beautiful experience of reconnecting, through love and acceptance to all of me. I have been set free to embrace true life in you, and for that I am eternally filled with gratitude!

Jesus: Every part within you, Lauren, is worthy of love and acceptance. Even the emotional distress from your past as well as all of your feelings around it. Love evokes even more love. For it is within the light of love that everything in all of creation is renewed, healed and inspired to embrace the freeing experience of being deeply connected to its creator . . . the embodiment of love itself.

AFTER

ST. THERESA'S PRAYER

May today there be peace within.

May you trust God that you are exactly
where you are meant to be.

May you not forget the infinite possibilities
that are born of faith.

May you use those gifts that you have received, and pass
on the love that has been given to you.

May you be content knowing you are a child of God.

Let this presence settle into your bones, and allow your
soul the freedom to sing, dance, praise and love.

It is there for each and every one of us.

THREE SIMPLE SONGS

In the midst of the divorce and cancer, I frequently sang three songs that I believe were gifted to me to help me maintain a sense of hope and love in the midst of the storm. I was moved to write them one year prior to the eye of the storm. Looking back, it is clear to me that God was comforting me before I knew that I needed to be comforted.

Come Closer

She's wondering
and searching
She comes back once again
with nothing but a broken heart and empty hands

Her soul is longing and thirsting
earthly waters that she seeks
leave her soul so hungry and so weak

Then she hears you call . . .
You whisper words of hope to her wounded soul
Calling her name . . .
words of love to her broken heart again

Come closer my child
Look deep within my eyes
Grab a hold, don't let go
I give to you abundant life

Come closer my child
Look deep within my eyes

and you'll find once again
the fulfillment of your longings deep inside

The poor girl calls
You hear her cries
Binding up her wounds
You breathe your life
into her brokenness

Forgiven now, she feels no shame
Healed by your pierced hand
Her heart surrenders to your love again

And she hears you call
With words of hope
You carry her home
Calling her name
Healed by love her
Heart no longer roams

Come closer my child
Look deep within my eyes
And you'll find once again
The fulfillment of your longings deep inside

My Soul is Restless: Wisdom from St. Augustine

You give freedom to my heart and comfort deep within
My Soul is restless Lord until it rests in you

You say my life is not my own, yet I feel I still hold on
My Soul is restless Lord until it rests in you

Too much to lose what should I do take
up my cross and follow you?
My soul is restless Lord until it rests in you

To the world my longings fled, turn
back now through tears I shed
My Soul is restless Lord until it rests in you

Living waters give to me, quench my thirst from all I see
My soul is restless Lord until it rests in you

Bread of life I long for more, I am hungry to the core
My soul is restless Lord until it rests in you

What's this love you offer me?
Heals my heart and set me free?
My soul is truly restless Lord until it rest in you

The old has gone, the new has come,
take my heart you have won
My soul is restless Lord until it rests in you

I am weak, you make me strong,
lost and broke you bring me home
My soul is restless Lord until it rests in you

All things now I do through you, love creating me anew
My soul is restless Lord until it rests in you

Life and love in you I've found,
feel so free no longer bound
My soul is restless Lord until it rests in you

Pressing on I grab a hold,
proclaiming love so pure so bold
My soul is restless Lord until it rests in you

You give freedom to my heart and comfort deep within
My soul is restless Lord until it rests in you

Am I Not Enough?

What a foolish thing to do
To rely on anyone but you
You hold the stars in the palm of your hand
You guide my heart to the promise land

You bring me up from the depths so cold
Move my mountains I take a hold
Of a love so sweet and a love so deep
Love of my life I finally meet

Then why, why, why,
oh why oh why am I still wondering?

From the cliffs of life you rescue me
Wipe mud from my eyes I finally see
The devil comes to kill and destroy
He twists my heart, I know his ploy

Pillar of fire you lead me on
Cloud by day I hear your song
Life and truth the only way
Coming back now I'm here to stay

Then why, why, why, oh why
oh why am I still wondering?

Surrender to Me I know your name
Don't be fooled by the world's game
I hear your cries
I know your heart
Come closer my Child am I not enough?

Know the price I paid you're not your own
Embraced the pain, endured the shame
Flow out of yourself and into my heart
Come closer my child am I not enough?

I hear your cries and I know your heart
Come closer my child am I not enough?

Why, why, why, oh why, oh why,
Are you still wondering?

ENDNOTE

[1] Williams, Margery, *The Velveteen Rabbit (Avon Books, 1922)*.

RESTORATION PICS

"I will restore to you the years that the locust has eaten" (Joel 2:25).

"And we know that all things work together for good to them that love God, to them who are the called according to his purpose" (Romans 8:28).

2018, Me with our 3 children: Johnny, KC, Kaylin.

Our big fat Greek Wedding October 3, 2009.

Big Fat Greek Wedding, October 3, 2009.

2012, Dancing with my dad.

2012, Dancing with Dean.

2025, Mom, Dad, and KC.

2024, Dean, Johnny, Melanie (daughter in law), KC, Kaylin, Ben (son in law), Therese (oldest granddaughter).

2023, Grandkids: Mary, Therese, Felicity.

2007, Dean and I. He's wearing my wig.

ABOUT THE AUTHOR

Lauren E. Miller, M.Ed, MSC, ICF-PCC is a stress relief expert, award winning author, motivational speaker, HRD trainer, *Edge God In* podcast host, and certified executive and life coach, Lauren facilitates fun process driven programs with guidance, support and accountability creating positive sustainable behavioral change in business and personal life.

Lauren has worked in youth and adult ministries for over 30 years. Through God's mercy, grace and strength, she uses her experience simultaneously conquering two of life's top stressors: cancer and divorce to help others destress and successfully move through challenges.

Happily, remarried and gratefully enjoying life in Colorado with a loving husband, Dean Fulford, three grown children and four grandchildren, Lauren is often found in the kitchen dancing to her favorite worship music or rolling around on the floor with her two dogs.

Lauren holds a Masters in Adult Education with a Certification in Human Resources Development | Advanced

Neuro-Linguistic Programming (NLP) Basic & Master Certification | Faculty Shift Leadership Training | Master Sherpa Executive Coach (MSC) and ICF Certification PCC | 2nd degree blackbelt World Tae Kwon Do.

She has authored 9 books, 3 of which are Award Winning:

- *Hearing His Whisper...with every storm Jesus comes too*
- *99 Things You Want To Know Before Stressing Out!*
- *Stop Letting the World Be the Boss of You! 25 Solutions to Refresh Your Identity in Christ*

Connect with Lauren:
Edge God In Podcast: http://EdgeGodIn.com

The Emotional Intelligence in Christ Project: EmotionalIntelligenceinChrist.com

Main Website: http://LaurenEMiller.com

Free Gift: Explore Lauren's 30 Day, 3 Minute a Day audio/visual Wellness Programs at Youtube.com/LaurenEMiller

Explore two previews of Power House Podcasts *from Edge God In.com Designed to Maximize Your Potential in Christ:*

1. Edge God In Podcast Week 17: A Negativity Detox: Step 1

Dear Lord I give you permission to override my negative thinking. Grant me the grace to cleanse out my thought life from all that is ignoble and unclean. Help me to have eagle eye vision to be able to tune into all that has a contaminating and corrupting influence

in my life so that I can by your grace remove it from my mind. Set me apart to be used for noble and honorable purposes. I want my heart consecrated to yours so that I am equipped and ready for every good work you call me too.

The focus for this study is a very timely topic and as we find ourselves surrounded with negativity. Let's face it, you can't give out to the world what you don't take time to master within. With that said, it makes perfect sense that the first step in a negativity detox requires high noticing around the negative elements you are allowing into your interior castle, those tenants that you are giving free rent to who are trashing your interior world, AND a willingness by the assistance of the HELPER, the Holy Spirit to take every thought captive and make it obedient to Christ. 2 Corinthians 10:5 is a worthy verse of memorization:

"We demolish arguments and every pretension that sets itself up against the knowledge of God, and we take captive every thought to make it obedient to Christ."

Learn:

The discovery of mirror neurons, in my humble opinion, is one of those biological wake up calls that reveals an essential element to the point of entry of negativity: our thought life . . . which ignites our emotional state of being. An emotion is simply your body's response to your thought life. Mirror neurons fire in the sender of information and the receiver.

Basically, anger evokes anger; love evokes love. Whatever you are experiencing emotionally triggers similar emotions in people around you. God biologically wired us to rejoice with those who rejoice and mourn with those who mourn. What was meant for good can easily be flipped to evil when we allow the emotions of envy, strife, bitterness, and judgment live under the roof of our minds.

Once you invite the Holy Spirit within your interior castle to help you master this space and detox your mind by evicting those tenants who thrive on negativity: drama judgment, accusation, shame, conflict, confusion, overwhelm, fear, doubt, worry you begin to reclaim the inner freedom of positivity Christ died to give you and you are then in a position to be able to step into being the light of the world, a city set on a hill to give light to all who see it.

Explore the Complete Podcast: *Negativity Detox: Step 1* with recorded replay and Edge God In Bible Study support materials please visit: EdgeGodIn.com. Join our weekly Edge God In Podcast, we welcome your insights.

2. Edge God In Podcast Week 18: A Negativity Detox: Step 2

Dear Lord, you are the LIGHT of the world, I give you permission to override my below the line tendencies that project "lights OFF" rather than "lights ON" to the world around me. I know that I can't give out what I haven't mastered within my interior world. Open the eyes of my heart Lord to tune into those phrases and verses that pop out to me reminding me of an opportunity to identify and adjust my perceptions and behavior to more fully embrace and live out your will in my life. This invitation to detox my life from negativity is not for the faint hearted. Strengthen my weak knees so that I can unzip my old self and zip up my new self, being renewed in the Holy Spirit with the gift of each new dawn. I want to be a city set on a hill and a light that outshines the darkness for you.

In the previous podcast: *Negativity Detox Step 1*, we explored high noticing around those negative thoughts and intonations we use with ourselves that dim our light for Christ. We now move into the experience of putting off those behaviors that fuel darkness in and around us as we step into shifting our attention on anchoring those actions that assist us in living a life worthy of the calling we have received.

Learn:

As we touched upon in the first step of detoxing negativity from our lives mirror neurons reveal an essential element to the point of entry of negativity: our thought life . . . which ignite our emotional state of being. An emotion is simply your body's response to your thought life. Mirror neurons will fire, triggering a similar emotional response in the receiver as put forth by the sender.

So, what does this look like when it comes to outshining the darkness? If you want to experience more kindness in your life, be kind. More love? Be loving. More compassion? Be compassionate towards others. This is a powerful blueprint in behavioral neuroscience that reveals the handiwork of God. Studies have exposed the power of a person's choice to remain in a place of love and kindness in the midst of outer negativity that is demonstrated by another person. The brainwaves in the sender are actually shift from the two-inch energy of the mind into the unlimited energy that radiates from the heart (The Heartmath Institute). Simply put, we have the ability to shift the brainwaves in another human being for a greater good simply by our choice for love and kindness.

Let's explore Ephesians chapter 4 and 5 which are jammed pack with behaviors that restrict our ability to shine, in fact that **fuel darkness** in and around us along with those behaviors that let our light shine for Christ.

Explore the Complete Podcast: *Negativity Detox: Step 2* with recorded replay and Edge God In Bible Study support materials please visit: EdgeGodIn.com. Join our weekly Edge God In Podcasts. We welcome your insights.

www.ingramcontent.com/pod-product-compliance
Lightning Source LLC
Chambersburg PA
CBHW050327010526
44119CB00050B/707